BLACK SUNSET

BLACK SUNSET

HOLLYWOOD SEX,
LIES,
GLAMOUR,
BETRAYAL &
RAGING EGOS

———

CLANCY SIGAL

ICON

First published in the USA in 2016
by Soft Skull Press
1140 Broadway, Suite 704,
New York, NY 10001

Published in the UK in 2018
by Icon Books Ltd, Omnibus Business Centre,
39–41 North Road, London N7 9DP
email: info@iconbooks.com
www.iconbooks.com

Sold in the UK, Europe and Asia
by Faber & Faber Ltd, Bloomsbury House,
74–77 Great Russell Street,
London WC1B 3DA or their agents

Distributed in the UK, Europe and Asia

Distributed in Australia and New Zealand
by Allen & Unwin Pty Ltd,
PO Box 8500, 83 Alexander Street,
Crows Nest, NSW 2065

Distributed in South Africa
by Jonathan Ball, Office B4, The District,
41 Sir Lowry Road, Woodstock 7925

Distributed in India by Penguin Books India,
7th Floor, Infinity Tower – C, DLF Cyber City,
Gurgaon 122002, Haryana

ISBN: 978-178578-439-2

Cover design by Tom Etherington
Interior design by Megan Jones

Printed and bound in the UK
by Clays Ltd, St Ives plc

Contents

PART SIX

PART SEVEN

PART ONE

PART ONE

1

The Fugitive

Alright, listen up, people. Our fugitive has been on the
run for ninety minutes. Average foot speed over uneven
ground barring injuries is four miles per hour. . . .What I
want from each and every one of you is a hard-target
search. . . . Go get him.

—Tommy Lee Jones in *The Fugitive* (1993), based on TV series
by Roy Huggins, whose successful television career begins
when he hands over friends and colleagues to the House Un-
American Activities Committee

M Y HEART IS pounding, and I'm sweating in my
Brooks Brothers blue pinstripe suit, broadcloth button-down shirt, Rep stripey tie, and buck shoes. A pair of
twelve-inch, one-and-a-half-pound steel alloy bolt cutters in
my jacket pocket feels as heavy as a .50 caliber machine gun
base plate. The army taught me how to squeeze under wire
to emplace Bangalore torpedoes, so it's easy to slice through
Universal Picture's perimeter wire fence in San Fernando
Valley where they've banned me for unethical, unscrupulous, underhanded behavior. I have earned the screaming
purple-faced rage of the studio's de facto ruler, story editor

Ray Crossett, and his demonic rages at anyone like me who deals behind his back. Overfed and overbearing, Crossett's bulge-veined tirades ("You pond scum! Cockroach!") intimidate even Universal's A-list producers, though technically he's only a mid-level employee.

My crime? While negotiating for one of my screenwriter's services I excused myself for a bathroom break in Crossett's office, crawled through the transom window, and raced to a public telephone to trade his offer for more money down the road at Warner Brothers. In a fury Crossett has set the dogs on me. Like fighter pilots, studio security guards scramble all over the lot, locking the gates. *Riot in Cell Block 11*. All it needs is a searchlight and a machine gun blazing from the guard tower; I grew up on prison movies.

I do this stuff all the time, it keeps me alive. I love the con, crises are my fuel. It's the best high . . . and anesthetic.

At such moments I take on false identities to make it through a tense day. Now I'm a Chicago Bears running back, nipping in and out of sound stages, bobbing and weaving behind equipment trucks, plunging into the maze of Universal's false-front sets: from a cardboard Algiers Kasbah's onion domes with rifle ports I make a flying leap onto a flat-roofed tower to slide down a standing plastic cobra to hide behind an Egyptian sarcophagus, tripping over a man-sized rubber tarantula and crashing through a straw-board wild wall straight into a cloth-wrapped mummy staring sightlessly at me. The studio's Keystone Kops, fanning out, fail to spot the criminal crouching under a faro table in a Dodge City saloon when I sidestep into a shell-shattered

World War I French village and dash across an alley onto a hot (closed) set where Tony Curtis and Janet Leigh, real-world husband and wife, are arguing with the director over a close-up for *The Black Shield of Falworth*—they must be wilting in all that fake armor and damsel-dress. Gosh, it's hot in the Valley. I'm dripping.

On *Falworth* the revolving red light freezes me like an army reveille: I snap to attention respecting the industry's First Commandment, to never mess up a shot. But I must sneak off this lot to call my client at home about his new quote (money), nail the deal before I'm nailed. Truthfully, I like lurking in the dark shadows of movie sets, like the sleeper "deep cover" spy that the US government accuses me of being. And I admire Ray Crossett for taking me so seriously, *Gang Busters* minus the sirens, although the studio maintains a battery of those for Soviet air raids if they come, which most people assume they will.

Sneak, thief, sneak. Duck under the fo'castle planks of *Yankee Pasha*, sprint smack into Joan Crawford—this freckle-faced woman in a white terrycloth robe, her hair turbaned in a towel, bent at the waist vomiting. Ah, yes, she's in *Female on the Beach* where my Jaffe Talent Agency, for whom I hustle, signed the director Joe Pevney but not the writer or Crawford. Pity, what a package. Even without makeup, her sickie soaking the ground, Crawford is a stunner. Those carved-in-marble cheekbones and large angry bloodshot eyes. She honors me with the immortal line:

"Get the fuck outta here!"

Mildred Pierce speaks! To me! My day is made.

Snaking in and out of the hangar-like cushioned doors of dark, cavernous stages, I trip over cables, flats, wild walls, hanging lights, and lynching-tree boom mics.

"LEGGO ME YOU PSYCHOTIC SONOFABITCH!"

"I'M CRAZY? I'LL SHOW YOU CRAZY YOU CUNT!"

. . . shit, I'm in a hot set in crisis.

Our rising Jaffe Agency client, Jack Palance ($65,000 per picture), is jumping all over our client Shelley Winters ($80,000), strangling her on a prop couch while her current boyfriend (unrepped by us) Tony Franciosa pounds on Palance's broad Estonian back, pulling at his skullcap while Shelley gurgles a death rattle, and our client Earl Holliman ($20,000) is piling on with the help of grips and gaffers, hauling frantically at the combatants. Franciosa hammers his fists, crashing down on the neck of Palance, who is throttling his female co-star. They're supposed to be starring in *I Died a Thousand Times*, a remake of *Colorado Territory*, a remake of our client Bogart's *High Sierra*, a remake of something else.

Zoom, I'm gone; someone else will have to solve our Palance problem. Last year, as Attila the Hun—or was it the Mexican bandit El Tigre?—he tossed his leading lady out of a second-floor window—or was it his wife? My über-boss, Sam Jaffe, who named the agency after himself (and why not), sighed, "Jack, such talent, such insanity."

Enough for one day.

Out in the clear, easy prey for mortars and studio guards, from experience I'm sure exit gates will be guarded so I belly flop under the wire fence. My dry-cleaning bills are astronomical on the days I infiltrate Universal, easy now, suck in gut, and away we go . . . up and away loping past Department of Water & Power pipe layers, over to my old Pontiac parked across the street and with a ticket in the windshield wiper, which I toss.

Flip the hood, twist the idle screw, check the baling wire holding up the engine, jump behind the wheel, pray . . . clutch, stick, and pray some more.

Westbound on Ventura Boulevard, a glance in the rear-view mirror, can you believe that Ray Crossett? Two of his guys still chasing me in a late-model canary-yellow Chevy Club Deluxe, making no secret of it. When I speed up toward Laurel Canyon, they're glued to my bumper. Crossett must be in some crazy mood.

❖

YES, I AM an agent. Not Joseph Conrad's Secret Agent or a CIA agent or FBI agent. But a talent agent, flesh peddler, ten-percenter, shark.

I work from a three-story Streamline Moderne building on Sunset Boulevard between gangster Mickey Cohen's haberdashery and the Villa Nova, where Marilyn Monroe and Joe DiMaggio have their first date.

This is my job, to sell, spit into the air and see it come down as money, make deals, spin webs of truth and deceit, cut more deals, close more sales, get caught in a lie, fall on my face, you'll never work in this town again . . . until tomorrow . . . and move on . . .

Because I eat only what I kill.
I love it.

❖

"*By himself a writer didn't stand a chance. It was all a matter of his agent. . . . But I despise agents.*"
　—William Saroyan

❖

"*Forty-five years I have been doing business with agents, as a performer and a director. As a producer, sitting on the other side of the desk, I have never once had an agent go out on a limb for his client and fight for him. I've never heard one say, 'No, just a minute! This is the actor you should use.' They will always say, 'You don't like him? I've got somebody else.' They're totally spineless.*"
　—Orson Welles, in conversation with Henry Jaglom

2

Farewell, My Lovely

You know, I think you're nuts. You go barging around
without a very clear idea of what you're doing. . . . I
don't think you even know which SIDE you're on.

—From *Murder, My Sweet*, directed by Edward Dmytryk and
written by John Paxton, both blacklisted

S UNSET BOULEVARD IS the second longest street in
Los Angeles and one of the longest in the world. From
downtown Union Station it curves west toward the Pacific
Ocean recapping much of my life's history. Let's imagine
we're a helicopter movie cliché that opens on a crummy old
car speeding west on Sunset from Chinatown, Jake, through
Echo Park up past Schwab's Pharmacy where William
Holden jumps out of Gloria Swanson's Isotta Fraschini to
buy his aging mistress a pack of cigarettes; on to The Strip
and today's Viper Club but yesterday's Sherry's Restaurant
where hired assassins who doubled as Los Angeles policemen put a hit on gangster Mickey Cohen, killing his bodyguard but only wounding him; and on through tree-shaded

Beverly Hills where Howard Hughes, then dating Yvonne de Carlo, crashed his FX-11 experimental plane into two private homes; just across from the tourist shrine of 810 N. Linden where mobster Bugsy Siegel was rubbed out in his own living room by either Murder Inc. or the Mafia or his girlfriend's brother or Meyer Lansky's gunmen (choose one); up past the broad green lawns of UCLA where as a GI Bill student I made all the right enemies; around Dead Man's Curve into Bel Air-Brentwood and finally the beach and Pacific Ocean where my two constant companions, FBI agents working from out-of-date Bureau file cards, are sure I'm still a "ComSub" (Communist Subversive), ramming my wonderful old Pontiac two-door off a Malibu cliff. Even today, to pacify my restless soul I still drive down Sunset to watch the sun-god die over the palisades.

Now bank that helicopter shot over Topanga, Pacific Palisades, and down the south slope of the Santa Monica mountains to my own little corner . . .

. . . and ZOOM IN to a three-story white stucco Ocean Liner Moderne building, at 8553 Sunset Boulevard, tel. Crestview 6-6121, between Ciro's and Mocambo nightclubs.

Hey, Head Grip, light this up in big sparklers:

THE SAM JAFFE TALENT AGENCY

I CAN'T PARK in the company lot because the three agency partners—Sam Jaffe, Mary Baker, and Sam's brother-in-law Phil Gersh—are embarrassed that my 1940 Pontiac—which I keep as a badge of honor—will disgrace their Eldorados and Chrysler Imperials. "Presentation of self" is vital for an agent, and my car, its backseat piled visibly high with political leaflets and radical junk, is an FBI agent's wet dream.

Until now, because I bring in business and am the agency's ace "fireman," a one-man high-pressure hose to extinguish unhappiness in fretful clients, the bosses tolerate my old wreck and me. But for now I circle up Londonderry Place in the hills above Sunset, past Mickey Cohen's exclusive whorehouse, and park under a jacaranda tree, and—mustn't be late for my own going-away party!—jog down in the hot sun. But when I get to Sunset Boulevard, those bastards from Universal Pictures, the security guards who've been chasing me all the way from Ventura Boulevard in the Valley, are parked brazenly right in front of the office sending their unmistakable message.

Except, they're not studio bouncers. Not with those government-issued fedora hats. I know who they are, and they have an even better idea of who I am.

SHOULD I INVITE them to my farewell party? No, they'd only eye-strip the guests, half of whom have just barely evaded the blacklist by quietly testifying or paying off the right people.

This job, for all its ethical contradictions and moral dilemmas, saved my life. But now Hollywood's Golden Age is dying, and with it a whole way of making movies. Soulless and educated like me, the New Smooth Men are replacing the old-style, vulgar, ungrammatical hucksters with their floral ties and ponies running at Santa Anita who made the deals who made the pictures that ruined and raised me. I've been breaking my ass to get assignments for sixty-four writers, and some actors and directors, policing their studio contracts, counting their commissions, listening to their complaints and threats to leave me, fighting (sometimes physically) to keep rival agents off my turf, and from time to time even rewriting their scripts. Maybe it's time to go and try to do for myself what I've been doing for them. Where and how is a wide-open question.

THE ROOFTOP PARTY's in full swing.

Made it, Ma. Top of the world. From here I can almost see my mother Jennie way out toward LAX airport near where she operates this small diner in a not-so-super supermarket. Sometimes, on weekends, I'll give her a break as a fry cook; it's a toss-up which of us is the more deadly Salmonella Chef. Her working-class neighborhood is a universe away from where I now stand on the pebble roof of the Jaffe Building with its near-views of Beverly Hills and Bel Air, doing what Mary Baker and Sam Jaffe trained me for: circulate and schmooze with clients like Peter Lorre, Vincent Price, Donna Reed, and Gloria Grahame—the latter a grateful gift from director Nicholas Ray for finding him a writer, a young Battle of the Bulge veteran, to start over from scratch and save *Rebel Without a Cause*, which Jack Warner was sabotaging because he hated its supposed attack on middle-class values. Jack Palance, Matthau, and Steiger are here, too. Steiger, whom I've wooed for months, half-forgives me for lying about getting him the unfilmable Mailer novel *The*

Naked and the Dead, and Lorre forgives me for trapping him in ghoul roles because he needs the money to feed his new baby and morphine habit. *Casablanca*'s "Victor Laszlo," Paul Henreid, is sweet to come say goodbye; he's one of the few clients who shares my condition of "star astigmatism," a mild mental disorder that confuses actor with role. I wish Dorothy McGuire were here, but I messed with her at lunch thinking she was the role she played as an anti-Semitic shiksah in *Gentleman's Agreement*.

I'll miss the daily craziness of serial phone calls, half-true deal memos, spun lies, doors slammed in my face.

Alas, our biggest money star, the very sick Bogie, is off making a boxing movie *The Harder They Fall* with our client director Mark Robson, currently under such blacklist threat that he's obliged like most of the tainted to make an anti-Communist film (*Trial*) to "clear" himself. The Bogart boxing movie is based on a novel by Sam Jaffe's nephew Budd Schulberg, a "friendly" (informer) witness in front of the House Un-American Activities Committee who named former friends, lovers, and comrades; the credited screenwriter on *The Harder They Fall* was Philip Yordan, the all-purpose "front" for banned writers. Who knows? In the blacklist game of disguises, the writer may be someone that Budd named.

And over there is my own coven, the poor schmucky screenwriters, well maybe not so poor at $1,000 a week, twelve weeks guaranteed when an average Ohio factory guy makes $100 a week with overtime if he's lucky. Here tonight is ever-reliable Danny Fuchs (*Love Me or Leave Me*), happy to work in sunny Southern California away from his cockroachy New York tenements; he made his reputation immortalized in the wonderful *Williamsburg Trilogy*. And Charlie Lederer (*Kiss of Death*), great western writers Frank Davis (*Springfield Rifle)* and Frank Nugent (*The Searchers)*, and Ernie Lehman *(North by Northwest)*, what a pride of high-wage talent! My seriously favorite clients, though, are the hard sells, the mutts like Nelson Algren, John Fante, Horace McCoy, and Jim Agee absent tonight, but over in a corner comparing quotes are the even lower-wage guys whom I tutor on *mitzvah* Saturdays.

All hands on deck, the thirteen other agents (most ex-military like me) plus secretaries and stenographers; the black janitor "Washington" (nobody knows his real name); the *balebos* himself Sam Jaffe, my savior bursting with ruddy baldheaded health; his partner and brother-in-law Phil Gersh (Third Infantry, Italy campaign); and my boss, teacher, guide, and personal "rabbi" Mary Baker, head of the literary department (and so much else) who is, not coincidentally, the older, married woman I have a crush on. She's my personal Florence Nightingale, that is if Flo wore Chanel suits and a rakish-angled Hattie Carnegie soft-brim hat. Mary's nursed me through so many of my costly mistakes. Tonight she looks more beautiful and butchier than ever in an open-neck Balmain silk shirt and houndstooth skirt, short at the knees, no New Look for her.

"Can I kiss you?" I ask.

"No," she walks away.

"You never give up, do you, Kid?" Our most patrician agent, tall and lean "Jonathan Buck," is watching us. "Your first day I warned you she's got a husband and kids and bats for the other team." Almost alone of Jaffe agents, Jonny— Princeton, Colonial Club, Office of Strategic Services ("Oh So Social"), face scarred by shrapnel or a childhood pox, nobody asks—is never seen juiced. Like everyone else he boozes hard, but the only visible clue is when his facial eczema, or whatever it is, blushes a little redder. Of all of Mary's "platoon guys"— her military trope—he's the most elegant agent trusted with the Big Kahuna studios, Metro and Fox.

"How do you do it, Jonny?" I wonder.

"Good breeding." He saunters away.

Jonny, ultra–WASP, does little to conceal his not-so-subtle anti-Semitism and is therefore amazingly successful with mainly Jewish studio executives who perversely share his prejudice and hence respect him all the more for it. Mary has three literary agents under her: Jonny, me, and "Zack Silver" (Navy minesweeper, Atlantic), my closest office friend, who has hunting and fishing rights, with rod and sometimes crossbow, on his Native American wife's Klamath reservation up by the Puyallup River. He, too, strolls by: "Our boss is way too old for you. Remember Jennings Lang." Lang was a Jaffe agent who had an affair with actress client Joan Bennett, who was producer Walter Wanger's wife, whereupon Wanger shot Lang's balls off in the parking lot of our competitor MCA. (A sympathetic jury slapped Wanger on the wrist for a brief term in county jail from which he emerged with the story for his *Riot in Cell Block 11*. Never waste material.)

Secretaries pass among us serving martinis on Mary's private Georgian silver salvers, and Zack and I are on about our fifth or sixth. I show it; he never does except for a slight nose blush. In the fading light Mr. Washington goes around checking to see if anyone has drunkenly tumbled over the parapet onto Sunset Boulevard. He's busy setting up metal folding chairs to face east toward the San Gabriel Mountains where, 300 miles away across the state line at Yucca Flat at the Nevada Test Site, the Atomic Energy Commission is getting ready to blow up a 28 kiloton above-ground nuclear bomb. In Las Vegas the tests are a tourist draw; casino operators print calendars with the dates and times of explosions.

Tonight I'm second banana to General Leslie Groves of the Manhattan Project.

I peer over the flowerpots down on the street where my ComSub crew should be passing out leaflets as planned, missing only one player, me. We call ourselves what the FBI tags us as, "Omega, alias Cell Without a Name," which sounds pretty sinister for a bunch of guys and one woman bickering over five-card draw.

DOWN THERE SOMEWHERE "Barney," Dorothy, "Jimmy," Irwin (sometimes), "Sparky," "Pete Pakulski," and "Joe Ferguson," but no longer "Ray Kovacs," lost to me forever, are running around slapping up No NUCLEAR WAR—STOP THE TESTS! posters. I'm probably too drunk to help anyway.

As the blood-red sun sinks over the Pacific, a cool breeze doesn't do much to sober us up on the Jaffe roof. After all, it's Friday night and most of the client calls are rolled up, it's all *gemütlich* because my going means one fewer agent to share the all-important end-of-year bonus, so there's real feeling behind the handshakes, hugs, secretarial lip kisses including tongues—see-what-you-missed-all-this-time? Mr. Jaffe grips my elbow emotionally. "*A glick ahf dir*—good luck, go be bohemian, but stay away from my daughters." Ah, so he knows?

My personal secretary Addy-with-a-y smiles glassily from a distance. She's a former Ziegfeld Girl with legs to match, can't type or take shorthand but like Mary Baker has been my crutch in the worst times. She's a single mother twice the other secretaries' age, uses way too much makeup, easily weeps (for me, herself), and is loyal above and beyond. On my first day we did it in the supply room because, as she explained, "All the agents sleep with their girls so let's get it over with and we don't have to obsess where and when, I've got enough worries, my son is an alcoholic at thirteen."

Up front there's a wooden table and metal chairs set up with a portable Zenith radio tuned into the KNX live broadcast of the bomb test. It's like a Hollywood premiere for us; will it be box-office boffo or a flop?

"Ten . . . nine . . . eight . . ." the on-site radio reporter counts down.

We sip our martinis. ". . . seven . . . six . . . five . . . four . . . three . . . two . . . one . . ."

The night sky over the Sunset Strip and the whole city beyond flares up, glaring red then whiteish white. The radio sprays static over us. Overhead, thin clouds reflect the furnace glow.

As one we raise our glasses to the east.
Someone cries: "It's a hit!"
We love winners.

3

Where This Story Takes Place

I N MID-20TH-CENTURY LOS Angeles—Raymond
Chandler's LA before Pilates and cell phones. Vernacular
architecture (diners shaped like hot dogs, gas stations like
UFOs), earthquake-defying wraparound-window hill houses
on fragile stilts, drive-in theaters. Cars with rocket-shaped
grills and tail fins, gas is twenty cents a gallon, women like
my secretaries (I have two plus a receptionist) wear petticoats and girdles. A brand-new Hollywood Freeway along
the Old Spanish trail of Cahuenga Pass cuts my daily commute to the San Fernando Valley studios.

The Korean war, into which I'm nearly drafted, has just
ended in a stalemate that costs over a million civilian and military lives including 45,000 dead or missing Americans. The
three-year-long bloodshed juices up the Cold War between
the two nuclear superpowers, Russia and the United States,
who have just fought by proxy in the Korean peninsula. A
permanent state of "national emergency" is declared.

World War III has begun.

It is in the opening skirmish stage already

—Headlines of *Life* magazine.

Nike missiles, armed with nuclear warheads, protect sprawling Los Angeles from a Soviet attack expected any minute. The glow from the Yucca Flat blasts can be seen from my office window. Nearby businesses have installed bomb shelters, but Sam Jaffe refuses, "What can Khrushchev do to us that Selznick hasn't?"

❖

FULL DISCLOSURE:

This is the story of my time as a young agent in Hollywood. I've taken liberties to compress time or hide some identities. Memory is fallible, so I've done due diligence by checking in with coworkers, accomplices, helpers, buyers, and sellers. Also with the "Omegas," our little subversive cell. I've consulted a diary I kept, and have used the archives at the American Film Institute and other libraries. A word about the Omegas: under different names I've listed all I can remember and those who have contacted me. Not all were present at the same time, although the core group remained remarkably stable under fire. In a world of betrayal there's absolute trust among us.

At this distance of time I've had to reimagine dialogue except when taken verbatim from contemporary notes, but have tried to avoid putting false words in the mouths of real people. I hope it rings true to the experience as lived.

The story is told in the present tense because it's how I lived it. Some names in quotes (" ") have been changed; this is especially true of the women, some of whom are today respectable grandmothers and may not want to be reminded of a time when they "leaped over the wall" of repression.

❖

BLACKLIST BLUES; BEING AN ACCOUNT OF THE EVENTS LEADING UP TO WHAT IS WRITTEN ABOUT NOW OR *HOW THE MOVIE VIRUS HIT ME*

I've been a movie balcony bug since age five when I ran screaming from the theater because the heroic German Shepherd dog Rin Tin Tin crashed through the silver screen to grab my throat. Ever since I've been unable to tell the difference between a movie image and what's real. But mostly I blame UCLA, where I was a post–World War II student, for what is a full-blown disorder. The Westwood campus, with its manicured lawns and manicured Breck-girl sorority girls (saddle shoes, bobby sox) is like going to class in the middle of a Busby Berkeley musical. Halfway between the beach and Hollywood, UCLA functions as the eighth sister of the nearby film studios known as the "Seven Sisters"— Metro, Fox, Paramount, Universal, Warners, Columbia, and RKO. Students burn to be actors, screenwriters, or directors. My steady date, an MGM ingénue, plays Jane in a Tarzan movie, and in my campus red group the children of the jailed Hollywood Ten of blacklistees invite me into their homes —a swanky Malibu house and a San Fernando Valley ranch—and let me ride their expensive Indian motorcycles up and down the beach. What a life it is to be a rich radical!

❖

"I walked with a Zombie. Had anyone said that to me a year ago, I'm not at all sure I would have known what a Zombie was. I might have had some notion—that they were strange and frightening and perhaps a little funny. But I have walked with a Zombie . . . It all began in such an ordinary way . . ."
—From *I Walked with a Zombie* (1943), written by Curt Siodmak

For me, too, it begins in such an ordinary way . . . with a gorilla, a blonde, and a gun . . .

4

Bride of the Gorilla

Bang! Pow!! The Detective Special recoils in my hand. Bang, bang!! I haven't held a weapon since packing it as a GI while being mesmerized by the second most powerful man in Nazi Germany, Hermann Goering, at the Nuremberg War Crimes tribunal. Today, on the *Bride of the Gorilla* set, in the old Mary Pickford–Charlie Chaplin studio at the tacky end of Hollywood, my blank bullets slam into the husky actor Raymond Burr who, yes indeed, resembles a version of the fat beast Goering. Burr crumples to the studio's jungle floor, play-dead.

Curt Siodmak, the writer-director behind the camera, yells in his guttural accent, "More shooting, Sigal! *Nach, nach! Sie schiest!* Rat-tat-tat. Crack crack crack! He's a *verrickter ape! Fertzig!* Crazy!"

Bride is shooting inside a small studio leased for cheap setups in a seedy Hollywood neighborhood miles away from the glamour. Siodmak is shaping his story around an overgrown plastic jungle left over from an old Tarzan picture.

A year out of college, captivated by my first movie job, I'm a twenty-five-year-old gofer, boy Friday, to the Assistant Director's assistant. Lucked into it, just by trolling side streets and asking. Thank you, Jesus, I'm on my way, hallelujah. Forgive me, Ma, it's nonunion, I couldn't pay the $1,000 bribe IATSE demanded for a union card.

Mr. Burr plays a plantation manager in Brazil who lusts after, then marries, busty, brassy actress Barbara Payton, Cloquet, Minnesota's gift to Hollywood. In the script she is married to an elderly husband whom Burr murders; Burr then drives himself so insanely jealous suspecting Payton is fooling around with the young village doctor that he morphs into a killer gorilla. The gorilla, in insert shots, is a redheaded Irishman named Russell wearing a hairy, moth-eaten rented suit; he moonlights as a bartender at Ciro's nightclub up on Sunset.

My kind of movie. With its movable wild walls, sweet-ish scent of sawdust and fresh plaster, snakelike tangles of black electric cable, portable generator's hum—everything *schnell schnell*—it's a perfect apprenticeship. Siodmak himself smears black Kiwi shoe polish on my face for me to play a "native boy" in a sarong skirt. A skirt?

Woody Strode, the bone-handsome African American UCLA athlete who along with Jackie Robinson helped to break the color bar in college football, is the story's native policeman. Since we're both Bruin alumni, on breaks I chum up with the big guy—but he takes one look at my blacked-up face and turns away in disgust. Hey, Woody, not my idea.

Barbara Payton, the cause of all this deadly jungle heat between Burr and the suave village doctor—bang bang!— is real-life tabloid meat. According to the wildly popular *Confidential* magazine that my mother Jennie swears she doesn't read, Barbara is sleeping with (at least) two lovers, ex-cop actor Tom Neal and aging star Franchot Tone, Joan Crawford's ex.

Mirroring the dark violent plot of *Bride of the Gorilla*, the two actors, Tom Neal and Franchot Tone, one a lowlife, the other a theatrical aristocrat, are poisonously jealous of each other. My duty, director Siodmak commands, is to intervene if by some mischance the two toxic actors collide on the set: *nichts, nil, nix* must slow down a skintight shooting schedule. I feel so honored to be working for a distinguished Hitler émigré like Siodmak I'd clean the toilets if asked (which he does). He got out of Berlin in '33, just in time.

I'd say yes to anything, even at 75 cents an hour, on a movie directed by one of the brilliant Siodmak brothers, Curt who wrote *I Walked with a Zombie* and *The Wolfman* and who adapts German expressionism into American horror pictures. I know this stuff because I'm a *Wunderkind* of screen credits, go ahead, ask me who are Perc Westmore, Leo Forbstein, Edward Willis, Tom Gunn? Ha, gotcha. The heart never has to be lonely in a dark movie house.

On set Mr. Siodmak's accent is often impenetrable to his actors and some crew, but my Blitz German from duty in Germany gets me by. I'm his useful idiot, quick and obedient, *jawohl, jawohl, Herr Direktor!* He's passionately practical on the set and wastes nothing, not even breath on me, whom he calls *Wunderknabe,* wonder boy, definitely not a compliment.

"You, *Wunderknabe,*" Mr. Siodmak points, "I zay more *geschossen.* And you, Herr Gorilla, crazier. Die crazier!"

Herman Goering, I mean Raymond Burr, slumps over deader than the green plastic foliage he topples into.

Everybody works fast and relaxed, it's not art but hardcore moviemaking. Yes, this is where it's happening, and I'm part of it.

Around our leading lady Barbara Payton, in tight jodhpurs and a deep-cleavage, half unbuttoned silk blouse, I'm all thumbs when the A.D. hands me a hair dryer to crouch behind Payton, out of camera range at crotch level, to blowdry her hair for a dramatic, typhoon-tossed close-up. Oh sweetheart.

One of my other duties is to rap softly on actor Lon Chaney Jr.'s dressing room—a sort of Portapotty on wheels—to alert him to hide the Old Grandad bottle when he's due on set. Lon, son of the silent's immortal Man of a Thousand Faces, plays a native police commissioner investigating the strange behavior of Burr whom the jungle spirits are driving mad, mad I tell you, mad.

My kind of movie, my kind of actors.

Anxious about delays, Siodmak tells me to "*Zuhören! Zuhören!*" (listen!) for the stage telephone if it rings to report that Mister Franchot Tone has arrived at the front gate when Mister Tom Neal is with Payton in her tiny dressing room, or if Mister Neal shows up while Mister Tone is with Miss Payton. I'm to drop everything and somehow keep them apart. Neal is a former boxer and will within days of the picture's wrap nearly kill the older man in a fistfight.

"IF YOU HAVE to," the A.D. says, "beat the shit out of both of them. You look in pretty good shape." Comes of weight-lifting sessions with my blood brother, Radovan (Ray) Kovacs, where we drain off the evil fumes of drinking sessions.

"You, college boy!" barks Siodmak. "*Spritzwasser* on Mister Burr's *Stirn! Schnell!*"

What's a *Stirn*? Ah, yes. Forehead. I spray water from a plastic bottle onto our lead actor's brow, and he politely thanks me. What a professional.

Russell in the simian suit removes his head and sprawls in a canvas chair beside me.

"No complaints but do you get the plot?"

Simple. Voodoo tweaks Burr into a mad gorilla.

He broods. "Mostly, on other jobs, I just rape the girl and then clock out, but the Kraut says no, just lay there dead, get my reflection in a pool of water, and no sex, I'm all dressed up with nowhere to go, right? I rent this rig per diem and my kids get a charge from seeing me goin' nuts on screen. Incidentally, I like your getup, Western Costume like mine?" He appraises me.

My thick wavy black hair is slicked straight back with goo, and my face is caked with Kiwi mud-brown shoepolish.

I doubt they'll use me, I say, because I look too "European."

The gorilla waves his paw dismissively. "That just means Jewish and Jews make good native whatevers. That old witch in the picture who puts the curse on me? She probably makes great matzo ball soup. They run the business."

This is the life, a native boy and an anti-Semitic gorilla shootin' the shit.

After the day's setups, still in makeup and skirt, I sweep up, empty trash bins, scan for Barbara whose crotch I've been looking up all day, no luck, so I'm off through the front gate onto the brilliant—real—sunlight of Formosa Street.

How I wish the gorilla was with me.

Parked curbside is an unmarked Los Angeles police car with its telltale four-way roof antennae—some disguise—and two of them inside. A uniformed cop is shooting me through the eyepiece of what seems to be a Keystone 8mm turret lens. Sparkle, Shirley, you're on camera.

That's the good news.

The cop with the camera lowers it so he and his partner can gape at me still in costume, skirt and mud shoepolish-makeup.

The cops exchange looks.

Mystic gods of chance, Mister Franchot Tone chooses this moment to be dropped off in a chauffeur-driven Alfa Romeo 2500 at the studio gate, and who should be lounging inside the guard booth chatting up the security guard but Barbara Payton's other lover, Mister Tom Neal.

By rights I'm off duty, but if there's an incident—Neal must outweigh a frail-looking Tone by a good fifty pounds—Mr. Siodmak will blame his *Wunderknabe*.

Just then the cop in civvies gets out of the LAPD car and folds his arms in a relaxed style on the roof while calling over to ex-cop Neal:

"Hey, Tom, none of that crap on my shift."

Tom Neal, throwing a smirk at Tone, ambles over to chat with his police chums. Franchot, whom I carry in my movie heart as the chignon-wearing aristocrat in the first *Mutiny on the Bounty*, the most expensive movie of its time, wisely retreats by summoning his chauffeur in the Alfa and smartly whisking away. Good thinking, old man. Situation *nil, nichts, nul*.

"Say there, beauty queen!" the uniformed cop in the car yells at me. "How about a date?" He throws me a girly kiss.

Mr. Siodmak sir, I swear I did my duty, no blood spilled.

But *alles ist kaput*. Across the street is a *different* unmarked car, this one a canary yellow Chevy Club Deluxe coupe, with two other guys, suits and fedoras, none of this LAPD-Hawaiian-aloha-shirt-concealed-weapon shit. The yellow Chevy carries an invisible PROPERTY OF US GOVERNMENT sign.

"Hey, fellas!" I trot across the street with a big hello to the Chevy, but my surveillance doesn't like being surveilled and they gun their car out of sight. In a skirt and feeling stupid, I'm absurdly alone, vulnerable, on a sun-baked Hollywood sidewalk. This past year I lost perfectly ordinary jobs, in a glassware factory and a record store, when the Chevy guys or their brothers dropped by to chat with the boss. It's 99 percent predictable they'll go see the *Bride of the Gorilla*'s producer Herman Cohen to ask their usual questions and that's it, I'm out. Poor Mr. Siodmak, a Hitler refugee doesn't need this trouble. What will he do without my Blitz German? Who will spray sweat on Raymond Burr's gorilla face? Can anyone fan the bride's crotch as conscientiously as me?

Goodbye, Barbara Payton, I hardly knew you.

❖

ACTOR RAYMOND BURR would be fine casting for Hermann Wilhelm Goering. My failure to kill the Reichschancellor will haunt me for years.

5

The Killers

G ERMANY, YEAR ZERO. Five years before *Bride of the Gorilla*.

In the movies it looks easy, but try sticking an M1911A automatic pistol with eight in the magazine and one round chambered down the back of your dress khakis, the weapon concealed only by a shortwaisted Ike jacket that hardly covers the bulge. I tug a little, which catches the eye of one of the 593rd battalion white-helmeted MPs on guard in the lobby of Room 600 at 22 Fürtherstrasse, the courtroom of the war crimes trial in Nuremberg.

"Give it up, pardner." The big rawboned MP corporal blocks my way to the high-ceilinged tribunal chamber. In a practiced move he slides his hand down my army pants to retrieve the pistol, politely disarms me, and checks my weapon atop a pile of other firearms in a side cloakroom with a receipt no less. Maybe I'm not the only homicidal GI here. I feel naked without my M19.

I'm here to kill Hermann Wilhelm Goering.

OUTSIDE THE COURTROOM is a landscape of still-stinking corpses buried under bombed-out houses. The people I see back at my (former SS) barracks in Frankfurt-am-Main are not the Nazis of Hollywood films but half-starved mothers and wives begging to wash our uniforms for a bar of soap or pack of Lucky Strike cigarettes (coin of the black-market realm), amputees, deaf, blind, deformed, self-pitying and pitiful victims, courtesy of B-17 and Lancaster bombers, sullen and shell-shocked survivors of the Eastern Front so grateful to be in the American, not the raping Soviet, Zone. I, armed with a .45, am their lord and master in this ruined land. Are these the same good citizens who watched passively their fellow Jewish citizens herded through the town square on their way to the death trains? I've known poverty in America, we're a welfare family, but this is off the scale, these people are out for the count. Mothers barter their daughters to us GIs. The black market defines Germany and the US army.

In the rubble I make several attempts to talk to elderly resisters, murder camp survivors, especially the frail old men putting up SPD (Socialist) and KPD (Communist) posters, but even if they speak broken English these walking skeletons are cold and angry and, believe it or not, still quarreling among themselves.

The streets are full of demobbed Wehrmacht soldiers, in rags or on crutches, and it takes an effort to keep from asking myself, was this or that one an *Einsatzgruppen* whose sole mission was to kill Jews? But it's hard to sustain, because at the same time I'm swept up in GI life, a druggy half-world of stolen cigarettes, twelve-year-old Fräulein hookers, massive systematic looting by officers, and the American Military Government's love match with former Nazi war criminals who easily lie on their *fragenbogen,* or denazification questionnaires.

I GO AWOL to attend the Nuremberg war crimes trial.

Behind me, at my barracks in Frankfurt, I leave work parties consisting of Jewish death camp survivors, the Displaced Persons who do the shit jobs for us (cleaning toilets, tailoring). Their bony faces set in a fierce scowl, the DPs are angry with me for refusing to smuggle them M1 rifles to take on their escape route to Bari, Italy and thence to the Palestine Mandate. I'm embarrassed by their predicament. I've never seen Jews so furious and determined. We American GIs much prefer the servile Germans. Who are these importunate, thrusting Jews anyway who promise to do my KP, lend me their scrawny women, please! give us at least one gun, and they curse me to my face, "*Azoy a yid?*"

Some Jew. It's all so fucked for the DPs whom I refuse to arm with easily stolen weapons. The Jews won't get justice in Germany. So, as a sort of compensation, a thought slowly forms: I am personally accountable. The real combat soldiers have gone home. I killed no Nazis. Now it's my job.

Inside the Nuremberg courtroom, where I'm in a front row of spectators, the once-obese Goering, in his unbemedalled off-white *Gruppenführer's* uniform, and I, in my Ike jacket and combat boots and unearned *Fourregere* looped through the shoulder strap, stare each other down.

He's the last living top Nazi since Hitler and the Gestapo chief Himmler are presumed dead. Reichsmarshal Goering, after Hitler the supreme authority in Germany, chief of the air force and instigator of the Nuremberg Laws dictating mass Jewish (and Slav, gypsy, homosexual, elderly) murder, signer off on the Final Solution of the "Jewish problem," architect of the first death camps—slouches in the first row of the trial dock, his uniform sagging on his cocaine-starved body.

HE'S UNFLINCHING AND indomitable. On my first day attending I hear him (via headphone simultaneous translation) run rings around the American prosecutor, Robert Jackson, by lecturing him with long pointlessly detailed answers like a high school teacher to a slow-witted pupil. He makes jokes, compares the enslavement of European peoples to the American slaughter of Indians, and swivels his large head around for his accomplices' approval, which he sometimes gets.

Goering slips off his dark glasses and polishes them against his cuff. Unlike the twenty-one other war criminals in the dock, he does not look broken, just bored.

He and I have been locking eyes for two days of grueling testimony including newsreel and slide shows of log-stacked corpses, mass murder statistics, Belzec survivors like ghosts turnstiling in and out of the witness box to give personal witness, Nazi low-rankers turning on their former masters in hopes of a lighter sentence.

He winks at me. Unmistakably. He has my number.

"Why does he do that?" asks the pretty young woman in accented English in the seat next to mine. She's a Belgian-born US Women's Army Corps translator, waiting for her shift, disconnected headphones dangling around her neck. During a break in the lobby she reveals that the Germans killed her family in Liège. She's matter of fact, like the antiseptic atmosphere in the courtroom. Forget Streicher, von Ribbentrop, and Speer, who populated my nightmares for so long, the only people who seem at all real are the low-level Nazi flunkies in the witness box, camp guards and assistant commandants eagerly, feverishly spilling dates, places, numbers to save themselves from the gallows.

The Belgian WAC asks me again if I have a personal thing going down with Goering. "He is said to be fond of you Americans, his guards bring him extra food," she shakes her head in wonderment.

In the afternoon session my eyes break away from Goering to scan the other defendants in the dock. Dönitz, Frank, Frick, Funk, Schacht, Hess, Jodl, Kaltenbrunner, Keitel, Krupp, Von Neurath, Raeder, Ribbentrop, Rosenberg, Sauckel, Von Schirach, Seyss-Inquart, Speer, Streicher: what a crew! Aside from Hess faking crazy, the others are not quite sure how to handle Goering, to applaud or pretend they don't know him.

In the dock these old comrades hardly talk to each other as if to show the Allied prosecutors: who are these criminals you have thrown me among? *Nicht schuldig.* Not guilty. I am innocent.

Is *nicht schuldig* even possible? After all, technically they are on trial for "crimes against humanity" that were not even legal offenses when committed; we invented the crimes after the fact. Is this kosher? True, in this emotion-drained Nuremberg courtroom the human monsters, so recently *herrenvolk*, are accused of atrocities beyond imagination. And yet—unshaven and shabby-suited—they eerily resemble my own father as he came in off the road hungry and penniless and hollow-eyed, or like those spooked and scrawny DPs in my barracks the men in the dock did their best to murder.

A jukebox tune from Spike Jones & His City Slickers runs through my head:

(accompanied by cowbells, gunshots, and whistles)

Ven der fuehrer says ve is de master race/

We heil! (phfft) heil! (phfft) right in Der Fuehrer's face

Are ve not de supermen/Aryan pure supermen/

Ja ve are de supermen/super duper supermen . . .

Shut up, Spike.

Of all the culprits, including "crazy" Rudolf Hess and the suave armaments minister Speer, for both of whom he shows open contempt, only Goering appears utterly at ease. Headphones on, he seems amused by these petty charges of genocide. When it's his turn to rise in his own defense he recites the same words as his co-defendants: "*Nicht schuldig.*" Bold as brass.

He grins at the judges as if daring them to believe his absurd claim of innocence. When he turns to look at his fellow defendants, they seem to shrink away from his coldly ironic gaze; they're intimidated by the once-mighty Goering who clearly delights in still exercising authority over them.

I can't take my eyes off him.

See me as he does: a US soldier in full-dress uniform with two rows of bullshit ribbons and high-shine combat paratroop boots. The fucker has me dead on.

I should have brought the smaller .38 instead. He'd be dead meat now, his brains spattered all over his off-white uniform.

Slowly, teasing, he winks at me again.

Sometimes he'll throw me a hippo yawn, as if to say, *Scheisse Juden ist nicht Soldat!* Shitty Jew thinks he's a soldier! I, Hermann Wilhelm Goering, have flown with Baron von Richthofen, won the Blue Max, and made the Third Reich my personal Wagnerian opera. What have you done?

His mocking gaze strips me naked of my sergeant's stripes.

During breaks the Belgian WAC and I make out feverishly, in an upstairs room of the Justice Palace, in her Jeep, and behind bushes in the Stadtpark. Then we straighten out our uniforms and hurry back to Fürtherstrasse 22, she to her headphones as translator in a specially wired seat, and I to my duel with Hermann Goering which he always wins. How can we think of sex here? Well, why not? The scuttlebutt is that the prosecutor Jackson is making it with his secretary. A dream of sex and mass murder.

On my last day in Nuremberg, in Room 600, Goering's baleful, omniscient eye seems to pick me out even when I'm half concealed in the spectators' back row. He has power over me.

Scheisse Juden ist nicht Soldat.

He knows me. All talk and no P38 Walther.

Even at nineteen I'm already a case. The only person who seems to know it is Hermann Goering.

P.S. I leave Nuremberg in such a rage that I hit another soldier who is slow handing me a billet chit for the night. As soon as I get back to Frankfurt, I bribe a buddy to cut me false papers ordering me back to America. Risking it, I tell the truth to my superior officer, Major Lovelace, a combat veteran of the 761st tank-destroyer battalion, who tells me, what the heck, if I have a chance, take off. God bless you, Major Lovelace.

6

From Here to Eternity

Montgomery Clift (as Pte. Prewitt): A man don't go his own way, he's nothing.

Burt Lancaster (as Sgt. Warden): Maybe back in the days of the pioneers a man could go his own way, but today you got to play ball.

—From Columbia Pictures's *From Here to Eternity* (1953), directed by Fred Zinnemann, who also made *High Noon* (1952). Lloyd Bridges, who plays Gary Cooper's cowardly deputy in *High Noon*, was "politically unacceptable" until with the help of lawyer Martin Gang he cooperated with HUAC.

I T ' S A N I C E spring evening in Gower Gulch, the corner of Sunset and Gower. I'm one of Columbia Pictures boss Harry Cohn's six readers or "story analysts," a terrific job with a good salary and great coworkers. I slipped into it by leaving town for things to cool off after the FBI came around to *Bride of the Gorilla*, just waiting for the right moment to ease back into the industry.

"What in fuck are you doing!?" screams bald and brusque Cohn while indulging his late-night habit of prowling the studio corridors turning off lights to save five cents of electricity. Next to J. Edgar Hoover, Cohn has the finest surveillance system in the USA, with hidden microphones all over the studio tuned into a loudspeaker on his desk in the Mussolini-sized, long-walk-to-the-tyrant's-desk office he had rebuilt after receiving a medal from the Italian fascist whom he admired. I have a sneaking affection for the bully Cohn because the few times I've been in his fairly terrifying presence, to "Scheherazade" (tell) him a screen story, a normal practice for busy uneducated executives who hate reading (and hence hate writers), he'd listened carefully, nodding at the appropriate story beats. No fool, he'd reached into his desk drawer to toss me a King James Bible. "Book of Samuel. Find me a Glenn Ford picture. David and Jonathan, rivals who love and hate each other, always good for a western. But nothing fag between these two!"

I was sure everyone had gone home. Then Cohn catches me red-handed staying late to use the story department mimeograph to crank out copies of a leaflet for Ray Kovacs to scatter over LA in his rented Piper Cub. Cohn is apoplectic with rage because I'm stealing "his" time and "his" equipment.

THE NEXT MORNING B.B. "Bubbles" Kahane, Cohn's VP in charge of security and cleaning up studio messes like Rita Hayworth's abortions and Sinatra's girlfriends, summons me to his lavish office whose flocked walls are plastered with life-sized glamour shots of the studio's stars like Rita Hayworth, Kim Novak, Judy Holliday, Montgomery Clift, and Donna Reed.

Every studio has its fixer like Bubbles Kahane, tasked to suppress newspaper scandals, bribe the stagehands union IATSE and the mob's Meyer Lansky & Co. in exchange for labor peace, and pay off the Los Angeles police.

Kahane, a big-shouldered, cigar-smoking, genial guy, is warm and welcoming to me as one of his lowly employees. More than polite, he comes around his desk to wrap a fatherly arm around my shoulder and nudge me into a big soft chair opposite his desk. He predicts a wonderful future for me at Columbia ". . . once we clear up our little problem."

Which is?

He sighs, "I was young once. Ideals. But think ahead. Your whole life." He actually adds, "Please."

Please? It's why I love America. None of this *Geständnis ablegen, Schweinhund!* "Confess, you swine!" stuff.

He uses a key from a chain on his vest to unlock a bottom desk drawer from which he produces a sheaf of stapled pages he pushes across to me.

A legal affidavit. Pages long. Buried in it is the life history of a stranger, not me, shedding tears for the unemployed, pity for the starving, duped foolishly into a Communist embrace, a full statement climaxed by an apology and repentance. Somebody's life history but not mine which, God knows, is "bad" enough. Whoever wrote this even got my age wrong—by ten years.

Just sign and I keep my job?

In a deep rich baritone he belts out: "*Names, names, ya gotta have names . . .*" He smiles. "*Pal Joey*, we just bought the film rights."

I ask him where he gets his information, and he replies that the studio has a couple of FBI agents on private retainer. Ah, them.

"Take a day off, son. It's your life," he grandly waves me out the door.

I need to talk to Ray Kovacs.

Jennie never gave me a real brother so it's Radovan, ever since college when, zonked even then, we'd fall asleep on each other's shoulder in class and if a plane flew over Royce Hall he'd jerk awake to scream, "PBY OA 10! FEATHER THAT FUCKING STARBOARD!" which is when I'd drag him out to the beach to cool off. He'd been an Air Corps pilot serving in Europe as an artillery spotter in an unarmored Piper L-4 Grasshopper flying low and slow over German positions to draw fire and radio back coordinates, which is probably why he's crazy.

Ray and I founded our little subversive group of pals as a Friday night poker game that morphed into, what can I call it? pranksters? undisciplined dissenters? The US government, dumb shits, has us down as ComSubs, Detcoms, and just plain traitors. Of us all, Ray is the impossibly good-looking one with jet-black curly hair, "Chinese" eyes, and a surfer's long solid body. He's a letterman on the UCLA wrestling team, which is handy in the jazz bar fights he provokes me to get into (anyway that's my story). And, of course, he's my girl Terry's "ex," which keeps it in the family.

Our favored spot is where Malibu Creek hits the Pacific, forming a tide pool where hundred-foot tall scaly monsters emerge with clawed hands, which is what Pepe Lopez Gold Label tequila will do to you every time.

Side by side, lying on our backs on the warm sand, I endlessly chew over whether to keep my job by informing. ("Names, names, ya gotta have names!") Is a compromise possible? Tell you what, I'll name the already informed on or the dead, what's the harm, you can't kill a corpse. Shading my eyes from the sun, I turn it upside and down like a child's kaleidoscope while Ray snores pretending to sleep, his naked arm snaking down to the Pepe Lopez buried in the sand. He yawns, finally gets up, brushes himself off and says, "This is bullshit. *Oushikuso.*" And walks off to get away from me, disgusted that I'm even considering it.

Back at Kahane's office at the studio, I flip pages of my pages-long "confession."

If I sign that's the end of it? I ask.

Kahane: "Then all you do is set forth, in your own words, a positive, forthright affirmation of loyalty to the United States of America and a ringing denunciation of communistic subversive groups and ideologies."

Who invents this language?

He senses my hesitation.

With a Jehovah finger he points to indicate Rita Hayworth, Aldo Ray, Lucille Ball, Evelyn Keyes, William Holden, Frank Sinatra on his walls. "They all signed! Or do you feel yourself so high and mighty more important than Rita and Frank? They're huge, huge." His voice rises. "See Aldo over there. A small town cop we made into a star. A star!"

All the Columbia stars are on his wall except the Three
Stooges. Larry, Moe, and Curly are Russian spies?

I draw a breath. "Mr. Kahane—what would Prewitt and
Maggio do?"

He blinks. "I'll check, but I don't believe I've ever seen
their names on our payroll as employees."

Why embarrass him by revealing that downstairs at this
very moment director Fred Zinnemann is shooting *From
Here to Eternity* where the two soldiers Prewitt and Maggio
played by Montgomery Clift and Frank Sinatra, respectively,
prefer to die rather than betray their sense of themselves?

Slowly, agonizingly, I push the affidavit, unsigned, back
at Mr. Kahane, and without a second's pause he mashes his
thumb on a battery of desk buttons whereupon two human
gorillas materialize out of the walls like Flash Gordon's
Rock Men.

"I guess this means I'm blacklisted, Mr. Kahane . . . ?"

His genial mask drops; I feel almost sorry for him, he
tried so hard to save my skin, really he did.

"Blacklist!" he meditates in a voice gone lawyerly quiet.
"By California code and the United States Constitution a
blacklist is a conspiracy and hence illegal. It does not exist in
our community. We obey the law!" He pauses. "Of course
there's no law against my phoning friends at other studios
and . . ." trails off.

For the first time he loses it. "WHY DON'T YOU JUST
OBEY THE FUCKING LAW!?" In a lightning move the two
security guards lift me from my chair and propel me by the
elbows, my feet hardly touching the carpet, down the hall,

past my former office, bum-rushed downstairs to the small front Gower Street lobby and into the street.

Out on the sun-seared sidewalk I look up at the building's second-floor windows where my family of coworkers— Jean, Maggie, Joanna, Ken, Arthur, and Estelle—stare down at me as if I've been dragged off to the guillotine. Their jobs, too, are on the line. Jean is crying.

ALL MY PERSONAL stuff is still upstairs. I don't want to join the so-called "blacklisted community," what a drag. Screw the Hollywood Ten, Trumbo and Lardner and Lawson, they salted it away in the good times, the director Edward Dmytrk probably got it right when he refused to give up names and honorably served his prison time and then, surprise! became employable again by testifying against his former comrades. Way to go, Eddie.

Under the warm sun, I take a pen from my shirt pocket and a torn scrap of newspaper from the street and write down **nine names** of friends, comrades, former classmates, and my girlfriend Terry.

I carefully fold the paper in my wallet. My future insurance policy.

A mournful, sweet, and poignant dirge echoes all over the Columbia lot and drifts out to Gower Street. They must be doing post-production on Montgomery Clift blowing "Taps," the army's lament for the dead, on the bugle he's been practicing:

Day is done
Gone the sun

From the lakes
From the hills
From the sky
All is well
Safely rest
God is nigh . . .

7

The Night World War II Ended

*L*ewis Raybin, an infantry sergeant, and I are showering
in the Army War College barracks in Washington, DC,
before heading out to get drunk on V-J Night 1945, victory
over Japan. Although infantry, we're both temporary clerk
typists in G-2 on stuff so top secret we can't understand a
word of it. Small bits of iron shrapnel tinkle on the tile floor
after working themselves out of Lew's much-shredded body.
He was blown up by an Afrika Korps mine in Tunisia and
then, wounded, went AWOL from the hospital to rejoin his
unit in time for General Mark Clark's massacre of GIs at
the Rapido River crossing in Italy. In civilian life he was a
lawyer and Democratic precinct captain in Brooklyn.

Soaping myself, I'm delirious over our victory.

"It's over, Lew! We won!" I'd slap him on the back
except he'd seep blood again.

"No," he replies quietly. "It's just starting."

The war against Germany and Japan is over. The war against us is just beginning.

RED TERROR ALLEGED IN SCHOOLS, HOSPITALS AND MOVIE STUDIOS—
Witness Testifies

—News Headline

8

Theatre of Blood

NO SURPRISE, THE Monday after Bubbles Kahane fires me, a subpoena arrives at my door commanding my prompt appearance at the LA Federal Building before the House Un-American Activities Committee in Room 600— somebody has a sense of humor since it's the same room number at the Nuremberg tribunal where as a GI sergeant I watched Hermann Goering defy his prosecutors.

After my act of chutzpah in refusing to inform, my nerves are shot as I sit alone and isolated on a wooden bench in the hallway, in Wrangler jeans and a good jacket and tie my clotheshorse Ray lent me. In a weird way I'm hoping that wearing his stuff will infect me with his natural insolence. I'm about to join the Legion of the Damned. My mother Jennie's mantra rings in my ears: *"You do what you have to do to make it happen."*

Through a porthole in the swinging doors I eyeball HUAC's living-theater inside, the courtroom lit like a stage production with carbon-arc Kliegs and TV cameras and angry shouts and the chairman's gavel pounding wood, bang crash whack! Flash bulbs, drama.

Abruptly the door swings open, almost knocking out my eye.

"Hey Kid, welcome to the club."

Paul Jarrico, the defiant witness who was shouting over the chairman, strolls over for a warm hug and handshake. In the blacklisted community, of which I'm now a reluctant part, there's a rigid status system, with Jarrico and other Academy Award winners at the top and the rest of us chumps way down. Of the unfriendly (hostile) witnesses, he's the most approachable; nights and weekends I help him lug 35mm film cans and sweep up his mid-Wilshire editing cubicle on *Salt of the Earth*, a pariah project he's producing about a strike of New Mexican zinc miners. His editing room is surveilled 24/7 by FBI who make no attempt to conceal it.

Inside the Federal building, Paul, former merchant marine with a rolling ship-in-a-storm gait, asks, "Where's your lawyer?"

I can't afford one, I say.

"Use mine, on my nickel." He laughs. "He doesn't expect to get paid anyway."

He picks up on my nerves.

"It's no big deal," he assures me. "Those bastards just want names." A quick look at me. "You don't have a problem with that, do you?"

If only he knew.

He puts his arm around me. "Cheer up, Mister Magoo."

Some of Paul's supporters emerge from Room 600. "Come drink with us after," he offers and disappears with them into an elevator.

I'm alone and feeling crappy. In the back pocket of my jeans is the sliver of paper with **nine names** including Paul's—who has been nailed so often he should get screen credit.

I will not be a loser all my life.

"You Clarence 'No Middle Initial' Sigal?"

A sheriff's deputy in pressed tan uniform is on me.

I get up. "Yeah."

"You're excused."

What? My hand was already dipping in my back pocket for names.

The bailiff says the Committee members are flying back to Washington for a House of Representatives floor vote; I'm dismissed for now.

"They can't do this to me."

"Life is tough all over," the bailiff shrugs.

The bastards have saved me from myself . . . for now.

9

On the Waterfront

Marlon Brando (as Terry Malloy): If I spill, my life ain't
worth a nickel.

Karl Malden (as Father Barry): And how much is your
soul worth if you don't?

—From *On the Waterfront*, written by Budd Schulberg
and directed by Elia Kazan. Both Schulberg and Kazan
name names of friends, lovers, and family to the House
UnAmerican Activities Committee. Actor Lee J. Cobb
(playing the mob boss) is banned until, pressured by family
troubles, he, too, agrees to supply names.

W HEN UNEMPLOYED AND unemployable in Los
Angeles, you find work for the despised and outlawed
on the San Pedro–Wilmington docks, offloading cargo cour-
tesy of the International Longshore and Warehousemen's
Union (ILWU), whose president, the outspoken leftist Harry
Bridges, knows what it's like to be surveilled up the kazoo.

The banana dock isn't far from where Ray Kovacs was
raised in the Croatian-American community that supplies
the wharves with much of its labor. So it's an easy commute
for him as we work as a two-man team of "banana fiends"

unloading ninety-pound green stalks from freighters out of Belize and Guatamala. It's a learned skill heaving bananas down to a Southern Pacific car on a rail spur without bruising the fruit.

You meet a better class of worker in San Pedro. While other stevedores are into the Racing Form and their *heroj junak* sandwiches of roast lamb and feta cheese, us banana fiends—often blacklisted types—take breaks lying in the sun reading Proust in paperback. Ray and I, stripped to our waists and hog-sweating, enjoy the workout. As (very) amateur body builders, bench pressing and doing Bulgarian squats, we pray honest labor will drain the poison out of our systems. Some chance: he's a coke addict, and my daily diet is Dexedrine, asthma inhalers, Tuinal, Miltown, and 87 proof White Horse in buttermilk.

At shift's end we stroll down the gangplank to the union hall to collect a day's wages, six hours at two bucks an hour = twelve dollars minus Social Security and tax. Behind the grill the maritime clerk points his nose over my shoulder. "Careful of the little guy, he thinks he's tough."

MY FBI HEROES, whom I've nicknamed Mutt & Jeff after an old-timey cartoon strip, are the only guys on the wharf with shined shoes. They're the lovelies who got me canned off *Bride of the Gorilla* and at Columbia Pictures and even, has J. Edgar no decency?, as a toilet cleaner at the Silent Movie Theatre on Fairfax. Jeff is the tank-built younger one with a linebacker's shoulders and a stone face staring down into a Rolleiflex camera snapping pictures like a boardwalk

Lothario. What's wrong with these guys, don't they go to spy movies where it's always a mini-Minox?

I shouldn't be surprised but I panic a little and smash my palm into Jeff's Rollei lens, which makes him unhitch his seersucker jacket to show off his manhood—the .38 service automatic; we're eyeball to eyeball at high noon on the banana docks.

Then . . . the Seventh Cavalry rides up like in a movie! . . . a glistening cherry-red Mercury coupe, power glide on a 350 Chevy engine, roars barreling along the pier and screeches to a heartstopping U-turn in front of the hiring hall where Ray is set (not for the first time) to save me from myself.

My girl and champion, Terry Allison.

Terry, née Tova Abramovitch, blasts the Mercury's horn with the first notes of Purcell's Trumpet Voluntary and sinuously eases out to let everyone get a good, exhibitionistic look at her tall, slim, bony-shouldered, high-breasted, pencil-waisted body in beach shorts and T-shirt. She drapes herself on the Mercury's hood like a porno model—which she's been—lifting one long leg, languorously teasing. What an entrance.

Mutt & Jeff can deal with the menace of world communism but not a transplanted New York model with a new nose and a fine body. Ray tosses her a fond kiss and then with his trademark bar-brawl grin, all teeth and no humor, pushes past the two feebs to trek up to his family's house overlooking the port by Vincent Thomas Bridge.

When I ease into the Mercury's passenger seat, Terry rolls off the hood and waggles her ass to the Feds. I never know what she's going to do or when. Here she is, even more choked with fears than me, and that's saying something, yet she'll go out of her way to court disaster; an accomplished shoplifter, she'll walk into Brentano's rail-slim and come out pregnant with half a dozen $15 art books between her long, long legs. She's game for anything, my girl who regularly turns over Bullocks Wilshire for Schiaparelli sweaters and Trifari pearl earrings and the thrill of doing it under the nose of store detectives.

Dread turns her on, which is why she's with me.

"I like you with your shirt off," she says, shifting the stick into first.

"Vice versa." I lean across to lift her T-shirt and kiss between her breasts.

"They're watching," Terry says.

"It's their job."

"Can't they afford sportier jackets? They creep me out."

"They're not hired for style sense."

But Terry is. At the moment, she's modeling for *California Apparel News* and before relocating from Manhattan to Los Angeles, before her nose job and while untangling from a husband who beat her up, she was a "Powers girl" who posed wearing Playtex bras in the Montgomery Ward and Sears catalogs (with her face usually cropped).

With me in the car beside her, Terry stomps on the gas and hurtles along the wood-plank roadway paralleling the water's edge while I drape an arm around her neck and draw her close, her tac at 2800 rpm as the Mercury is running out of track. A looming gantry marks the end of the road.

For whatever reason we like to terrify each other.

I went for Terry when Ray and I shared a room and she walked in one night and sat on his bed with a look of such tenderness and lust for Ray that right then I had to have her, so when the Air Force called him back (before they kicked him out again because they can't have a Red fighting the Reds), Terry was mine.

The onrushing skyscraper-high gantry fills the windshield. The high-up cab operator frantically waves us off but instead of braking Terry very calmly inserts her gearshift hand down my jeans.

We're right on top of the gantry.

10

Holding My Nose and Praying

H AND IT TO J. Edgar Hoover, he hangs on like a crazy pit bull. Where can I go where the FBI can't find me?

My present situation is dire. I can't pay my rent on a room near the freeway, and sometimes Dumpster dive for leftovers in the back of Nate 'n Al deli on Beverly Drive. Even so I make time to vote for Ike Eisenhower as president over the Democratic darling Adlai Stevenson. My girl Terry, a New York–born leftie, slaps my face in fury over my transgression. Nerves are taut. Sen. Joe McCarthy, advised by his sexually weird aide Roy Cohn, who also prosecuted the "atomic spies" Julius and Ethel Rosenberg, has found a winning issue in accusing Eisenhower and World War II Chief of Staff George C. Marshall and your uncle and aunt as Communists, traitors, and homosexuals in that order. "McCarthyism" is born, along with UFOs sighted over the nation's capitol, Jo Stafford's hit "You Belong to Me," and

Joe Stalin showing McCarthy how to do it with his Soviet show trials of Jewish doctors, including his own.

Broke and carless, unemployment expired, fired "for cause" from even the lowest profile jobs (toilet cleaner, cement mixer), and my old prewar Pontiac held hostage at a friendly Texaco station, I'm aimlessly strolling down Sunset Strip under a blazing hot sun, a fucking pedestrian, when the driver of a passing Studebaker bullet-nose Champion hails me. Anita, a six-foot olive-skinned beauty, calls through the open car window:

"Hey there, Tom Joad, if you're crazy enough to want it, I got a job for you." Anita, who sleeps with me when she isn't husband-hunting on Zuma Beach in a faux leopard-skin bikini, works as a secretary up the street at the prestigious Sam Jaffe Talent Agency, which needs a replacement for an agent they just dumped, she says.

I've sunk so low?

"Suit yourself. You're a liar and a rat, and if your relationship with me is anything to go by—you'll make a perfect flesh peddler." Off she drives, letting me stew in the sun, just another Los Angeles lost soul.

Agents do what?

"They sell the writer—or sell out the writer—depending on who the agent values most, seller or buyer," advises my friend and comrade, the banned screenwriter Paul Jarrico, in his cramped editing room off Wilshire Boulevard where he cuts dailies of *Salt of the Earth*. With too much time on my hands, I help with the crap work. Paul was sometimes agented by the Jaffe office, which dropped him when the House Un-American Activities Committee subpoena came.

"If you have to ask what an agent does," Paul says, "maybe God doesn't mean for you to be one."

But God doesn't pay my rent.

11

Liar, Liar

I 'VE YET TO tell the truth to get a job.

Practically from the cradle my mother Jennie, currently working at a Catalina Swimwear sweatshop on a 4-thread overlock machine for a buck seventy five an hour, drilled into me her survival mantra: "*You do what you have to do to make it happen.*"

Today my interview at 8553 Sunset is with Mary Baker, the Jaffe agency's hiring master and literary honcho.

First, I check myself out in a shop window. Who am I today? The reflection says I'm twenty-five with a "boyish" look—is that good or bad? Nearly six feet, fairly packed with muscle from all those weight-lifting sessions with Ray, a thick head of jet-black hair just like my dad before he vanished from our life, a face I have to work on to make it look harder and more assertive, no visible scars and a lousy dress sense—must work on that, too. Friends say when I wear my horn-rim glasses I look like a tone-deaf Buddy Holly. You don't want to hear my "That'll Be the Day." As the sun cannonades off the white-stucco walls of the agency building, on the corner of La Cienega and Alta Loma Road with downhill-racer views of the Baldwin Hills oil fields and on a clear day out to the ocean, I hitch up my (borrowed) pants mimicking James Cagney, puff out my chest like Robert Mitchum, and take on the persona of a wisecracking Clark Gable, my movie fathers. How else can one live, except by putting on layers of identities and wearing a life-mask of my favorite movie stars, a rough draft of how to function in the real world? Otherwise, I'm invisible to myself and others.

With a John Wayne strut and an Errol Flynn grin I muscle through the Art Deco double doors where . . .

. . . it feels like I've stepped onto an ocean liner. The Jaffe Agency floor plan with offices extending from a central corridor looks nautical; even the windows are circular like portholes. A tall, tawny receptionist with a sweater and twin set and a girdle-enforced wiggle takes me upstairs via a spiral metal staircase to the upper deck of cabin-like offices with sunlight streaming in from large windows port and starboard. Two parallel rows of female typists in the secretarial well, like oarsmen in a Roman galley, are attached to cabin-like offices where strange men in suits work the phones.

❖

Do what you have to do to make it happen.
The interview goes well.

The reason is that Mrs. Baker instantly demolishes my fabrications. "Kid, you're horseshit and a yard wide. But I kind of like your style." Kid, yet.

Neither of us seems embarrassed by the lies I've told her. This tells me all I need to know about an agent's world.

All she wants to know is, "Are you of the Tribe?"

Her East Coast accent. "*Ahr yew of the trahb?*"

Pardon?

"*Redstu Yiddish?*"

I shrug noncommittally.

"Learn," she snaps. "It's how business is done around here."

She's wearing a small silver Crucifix around her neck, and when my eyes drop to her bosom she says in a low throaty cigarette-rasp, "Bryn Mawr, Katie Hepburn was in my class. She's a sometime client when we can stand each other, get your eyes off my tits, I'm high Episcopal, none of that pigshit low church trash."

Without prompting she adds, "The Jews saved my life. If Sam Jaffe hadn't hired me as his receptionist, at fifteen dollars a week, I'd be in Bellevue's alcoholic ward or throwing myself out of a Park Avenue penthouse window because I'd married a limpdicked stockbroker who wears two-tone wingtip shoes. *Danke Gott fur die Yiddishe volk.*"

Mary Baker fits a Pall Mall cigarette—my mother's brand!—into a bone-ivory holder and takes a long drag at a jaunty angle like president Franklin Roosevelt used to pose for photographers.

Why is she telling me all this? She's already exposed my résumé as a big fat lie.

Her antique Gatsby-era phone rings and is picked up by her small-boned female assistant Cricket, who hands it to Mrs. Baker. "Selznick. Again."

On the phone Mary Baker is all smiles: "Da-vid, *mein guten cha-ver, du bist in guten gazinteh?*" She roars with laughter at something he says.

Mrs. Baker keeps her eyes on me while she banters with David Selznick. Then, taking me unawares, she reaches across the desk to toss the phone at me, holding her hand over the receiver.

"Selznick wants our writer Charlie Lederer. Tell him he can have Charlie on a two-fer if he hires Joe Cotton for Jennifer's next picture. Charlie's quote is 1,500 on a ten-week guarantee. Let's see what you're made of. "

Last month on the San Pedro docks, I'd made $60 a week.

❖

SELZNICK'S ANGRY SQUAWK can be heard from across the room.

I stare at the phone.

Me, impulsively, into the phone: "Sir . . . Sir. Mister Selznick . . . um, Mrs. Baker . . . er, excused herself to the ladies . . . No, I'm not the office boy."

You have to understand, David Selznick is Zeus who gives birth to gods. He made *Gone With the Wind, Nothing*

Sacred, A Star Is Born, all the pictures I grew up on. He *created* my mind.

I silently mouth to Mary Baker "What do I do?" She is poker-faced. Bitch.

What choice do I have?

Me, picking numbers out of the air: "Um. Eighteen hundred a week is Mr. Lederer's new price. She already quoted fifteen hundred? And you want him for seven fifty? Please Mr. Selznick." I am a screen credit prodigy having memorized the small print practically since infancy. Sydney Guillaroff or Rudy Maté or Lodge Cunningham? Yakima Canutt? You might as well not know who the Pope is.

Selznick sputters. He demands Mrs. Baker. I take a final cut at the plate.

Me: "Excuse me, Mr. Selznick, of course you know that Mr. Lederer wrote *Lady from Shanghai* which made an actress out of Rita Hayworth. He'll do the same for Jennif . . ."

A bridge too far.

Rage at the other end.

I hold the receiver away from my hurting eardrum.

Cricket rolls her eyes, and Mrs. Baker gently lifts the phone from me. Her voice low, soothing. "Sure, he's arrogant. A born *pusherke.* Reminds me of you back when." Pause. "Of course we can work out the numbers . . ."

Blah blah blah, love to Jennifer, hang up.

Mary Baker narrows her blue-shadowed eyes at me, holding my life in the balance.

A confirming glance from Cricket, her assistant and clearly her second half, and Mary Baker says, "I won't let you near the quality studios Fox or Metro. Or Paramount or even RKO. You'll handle the Valley—Universal, Warners, and Republic."

I'm hired?

She leans back in her Windsor-style armchair.

"I told you, Kid. Pure horseshit without breaking a sweat. . . . Cricket, I'm thirsty."

Her assistant goes to the corner mini-fridge and brings out a Chinese-lacquer Thermos jug. Mrs. Baker pours herself a tomato-red Bloody Mary. I can smell the vodka from here.

"Drink?" she offers.

Eleven in the morning. Early for me.

"It's late for me," she even laughs like her client Barbara Stanwyck in *The Lady Eve*.

I can't take my eyes off her. She knows it.

She empties her cut-crystal glass in two swallows.

That's it?

"*A bi gezunt*," she says. "Except, don't you ever again trash an actress the producer is sleeping with like Jennifer and David. And one more thing: don't you ever lie to me again. *Fershtayist?* Understand?"

She adds, "'*Trust each other or die*.' That's Auden, son."

"Ma'am, it's '*love each other or die*'."

She lifts her marvelous chin. "You're literate! Sam Jaffe will love it. As of Monday you're on the payroll."

This woman is officer material.

I'm at the door when she springs it on me.

"Are you clean?"

I feign ignorance.

Before I can lie she surprises me. "Forget it, I don't want to know."

I'm released.

Not quite. My hand on the knob she says, "By the way, what's on your dog tags?"

"36 929 935," snapped out from memory.

"Good," she's satisfied. "My thirteen boys are all ex-service. My platoon. Combat experience. Comes in handy." Proudly she reels off Jaffe employees with their medley of battle scars; names fly by me, this one North Africa, that one special operations, a string of battle names, Navy mine-sweeper, Marines, paratroops, combat engineers, D-Day Omaha beach, B17 tail gunner.

Time to go. Cricket's leg swings back and forth like a crazy pendulum.

I open the door and come face to face with . . .

. . . "Mad Dog" Earle and Sam Spade . . .

I will *not* faint. Who is this aging, bag-eyed man with a bent-over slouch in a blue cardigan who looks like the nightshift manager of a third-rate night club—but isn't that exactly what Rick is in *Casablanca*? Humphrey Bogart, Jaffe's client, is short. My eyes shift down at his shoes: no lifts at least.

"Sorry, Mary," a cultured sandpaper voice, "they didn't say you were busy."

"*Entrez*, Bogie," Mrs. Baker swivels around. "Say something to impress the kid. Look at him, he's practically having a heart attack."

Bogart scowls, grunts, and delivers on cue, "'*Get away from that phone, Major Strasser.*'"

My other curse is total recall of movie dialogue. "Excuse me, sir, but isn't it, '*Put that phone down!*' and no Major Strasser?"

Bogart, challenged, concentrates: "'*I was born when she kissed me. I died when she left me. I lived a month while she loved me . . .*'" Ha! Got ya!"

Can't help myself. "Mr Bogart, the line is '*I died when she left me, I lived a few weeks while she loved me . . .*'" From my all-time favorite Bogart movie *In a Lonely Place*.

Mrs. Baker whoops with laughter. "He got you, Bogie!"

Grumpy. "Who remembers?" He whirls on me and points his finger like a gun. "'Drop the gat, Louie!' Ha! I got you again. I never said it!"

He slumps in the chair by Mrs. Baker's desk and gives a little laugh. "Pedantic little shit, isn't he?"

And so ends my first day as a Hollywood agent.

12

Pulling an All-Nighter Cramming for the Job I Bluffed Into

I T'S MINE TO lose.

In my hot cramped room under the Santa Monica Freeway, I study Budd Schulberg's novel *What Makes Sammy Run*, a learner's manual on how to be a successful agent. Like me, the antihero Sammy Glick has defective moral brakes. I wonder if Schulberg, a screenwriter and novelist, ever read his own book, because in real life he became his own Sammy, betraying friends. Easy now. Schulberg is the nephew of my new employer Sam Jaffe, a prince of the royal blood. "It's Hapsburgs and Romanovs," Paul Jarrico says, "everybody in Hollywood is somebody's relative even when—no, especially when—they declare war on each other."

On the pull-down Murphy bed my girl, Terry Allison née Tova Abramovitch, takes the novel out of my hands

and tosses it on the floor. "You'll do just fine." She fits herself under me and wraps her legs around my naked back.
"Cheat. Pretend. Scam." She arches herself. "Do what comes
naturally."

13

O Brother, Where Art Thou?

R AY KOVACS AND I are celebrating my future paycheck on a last free weekend before I go to work at the
Jaffe Agency.

In a rented Piper Cub we're diving at 2,000 feet over
Beverly Hills, swooping and jinking while I lean out of the
Plexiglas window tossing out anti-McCarthy leaflets over
the Hollywood film factories—and leaning out to watch
them flutter down on the scalloped Bel Air landscape of the
rich and famous.

"Save some for the Orange County zombies!" Ray yells
into my half-frozen ear as he pilots the plane west toward
the Pacific Ocean, banks over Huntington Beach and heads
south (oh my stomach!) for me to fling more paper over the
flatlands of Anaheim and Costa Mesa.

I'm smashed on Montezuma Gold because Ray doesn't
carry a radio or parachutes ("Silk is for sissies"). Ray, whose

real name is Radovan—former US air corps Grasshopper L-4 pilot in the European theater—is flying by the seat of his pants which he's now unzipping as he waggles the joy stick between his knees. He claims to do his best flying on cocaine, "just like Freud and Sherlock Holmes."

With trousers around his knees and sideslipping all over the skies of the Southern California basin, Ray slides open the canopy window to scream into the rushing wind, "Turn off your fucking TVs, you morons!"

Then he grabs my free hand and wraps it around the control stick. I drop hundreds of altitude feet in the changeover. He twists around in the cockpit so his rear end is to the open door and takes a shit all over Orange County. You wouldn't believe that at 120 mph brown turds flying out the door in a cold air stream would stink up the small cockpit, but they do. Ray wipes his ass with one of my leaflets—hey, have respect, I wrote it!—and drunkenly grabs the stick from me.

There they go, my babies, like snowflakes over a sunburnt terrain, the only writing I've managed to produce at the ripe age of twenty-five. Norman Mailer was twenty-five when he wrote *The Naked and the Dead*; on the other hand J. D. Salinger was an old man of thirty-one when *The Catcher in the Rye* came out last year.

Ray is flying us through militarized air space with its scrambling F-80s and Nike missile sites pointing skyward at us. Will their radar operator mistake us for Stalin's ICBMs and shoot us out of the sky?

The Piper's motor sputters. I swallow hard. I'll bet Ray has forgotten to gas up, I'll bet.

He looks over at me. We've been through a lot together. He blinks his eyes in semaphore and chuckles, "You're such a worry wart. God Is My Co-Pilot."

He puts the plane into a sudden 3-G dive straight down, the joystick forward hard.

He shouts, "Who rules?"

My jaw hurts, my cheeks flap in the downward wind rush. Together we scream into the rushing wind: "OMEGAS RULE!"

14

Who Are the Omegas?

"THE CELL WITHOUT A Name alias Omega" is how the FBI classifies us, I learn years later from a Freedom of Information request. Put simply, we're eight marginal youngish men and one middle-aged woman who began as an ordinary Friday night five-card stud, high-low nothing wild game at my place and, helped by Comrade Johnny Walker Black Label, spontaneously invent ways of sabotaging, pranking really, J. Edgar Hoover, a mythical warlord in a faraway land.

WE HAVE NO illusions about our "effectiveness." Each of us has been blackballed for one reason or another: Ray discharged from the US Air Force; "Jimmy," a "conchie," incarcerated at Lompoc Minimum Security for refusing military service; "Barney" fired from a hospital residency; self-taught lawyer Irwin Edelman constantly arrested for making speeches to test the First Amendment on a soapbox in Pershing Square; "Sparky" excommunicated by his own dockers' union for speaking up for black longshoremen; "Joe Ferguson," a French horn player, works studio gigs under an alias because his girlfriend's father, who opposes the love match, told the FBI about him; Dorothy Healy, Southern California's Party leader, the "human face of communism," in and out of jail much of her life, disapproves of our "lack of discipline" but likes our energy; "Pete" (Bronze Star, two Purple Hearts) lost his teaching job in a Valley high school. Politicswise, only Dorothy and Ray are currently Party members. Sparky is a Trotskyist of the Shachtman persuasion. Irwin is a hard-core libertarian. Jimmy is a Quaker pacifist. Barney and Joe, who knows? Pete, 11th Airborne paratrooper, is an "ex" Red and so am I as of several years ago. Ray (180 pounds), Pete (200), and I (170) are the designated on-call Movement bodyguards when Paul Robeson comes to town or a storefront meeting place is torched.

We depend totally on one another for mutual support in a lonely time.

Out there the rest of the country is prospering, but we're still at war with the government and ourselves.

We are not fearless but as scared by the same nuclear warhead that hangs over everyone else, plus knowing that we have bull's-eyes on our backs as targets for the proposed "Emergency Detention Act" (S.4037), pushed by liberal senator Humphrey, to arrest and deport us subversives to concentration camps. As my mother used to say about a certain Danubian ethnic group, if you have one for a friend you don't need an enemy; the same goes for liberals who want to head off Senator McCarthy by doing the same thing only first and better.

The Omegas object to my friendly chats with the Federal agents who drop in. But I'll talk to anybody. What have I got to hide, aside from my life?

Anyway, the Feds have me nailed. I'm not innocent.

15

The FBI Story

On Sunday morning he left the house. He couldn't be going to work. Since he was a Communist, we knew he wasn't going to church.

—Jimmy Stewart as Federal Agent Chip Hardesty in *The FBI Story* (1959)

I T GOES LIKE this.

A warm summer evening. My apartment screen door, like a priest's confessional lattice, is off the hook.

Knock, knock!

My FBI shadows. They never give up.

"Hey, Clancy, congratulations on the new gig. Great going."

No tax dollar is wasted. They show up whenever and wherever I get hired. In this case even before I start the job.

They call themselves "Mr. Wilson" and "Mr. Jones" but to me they're still Mutt and Jeff, the Bud Fisher cartoon strip about a tall and short pair of buffoons. Mutt, the senior FBI agent, looks like the actor John Carradine (Preacher Casey in John Ford's *The Grapes of Wrath*), a human cadaver with colorless eyes; Jeff, his junior partner, has a Panzer tank physique also with a fixed over-produced stare. Fedoras off, bareheaded, they wear Marine Corps high-and-tight haircuts, two-button sharkskin sports jackets, knotted ties, square-toed brogue shoes. They could be working for IBM or Xerox with their mandatory dress code.

Courteously, they never raise their voices or a hand to me, though Jeff, the little bulldog, still has this habit of acci-dentally-on-purpose exposing his shoulder-holstered can-non. What, he's going to shoot me on my own doorstep?

Definitely I am mindfucked because I look forward to these FBI nights. These guys center me.

Through the screen door:

"Now, Clancy?" Jeff.

"Not now, fellas. Lighten up. You don't want to wake the neighbors." Which is exactly what they do want to do.

"What about it, Clancy?"

Me: "*Nicht, nein, nyet, non . . .*"

Jeff interprets, "That '*nyet*'. It's Russian."

They kill me.

❖

I WISH THEY'D understand that I had been a Junior G-Man by sending in Quaker Oats box tops and proudly wore my official tin badge and had J. Edgar Hoover's con-gratulatory letter pinned to the wall. If only they knew how much I *want* to be a good American and do my part in the global struggle against evil.

Jeff predicts, "You'll come in. Sooner or later. You all do. Eugene did. And Lois."

Eugene, in a hospital bed after his cancerous arm was amputated when the feebs showed up to interrogate him.

I say, "Lois?" Impossible. A strict one-hundred-percenter like her. Never, not Lois. Really?

Jeff: "Come on, don't be a party poop. Help us clean up our files."

Mutt, the John Carradine one, pulls out my 3x5 file cards from his inside jacket pocket. At least it's not a .38.

"We know you handled top secret material."

"SAY WHAT?"

"And you were observed at the Soviet embassy," Jeff reports.

Oh right, years ago on V-J Night war's end a wounded buddy Lew Raybin and I staggered around Washington, DC, kissing all the Russians we could find in uniform and some of them were even women.

Fellas, I'm really sleepy.

IN A SGT. Joe Friday monotone Mutt builds a solid case from his file cards where he alleges I am:

(a) The "sexually deviant," left-handed, lisping ring-
leader of Omega, alias Cell Without a Name, that plans
and executes illegal subversive acts. Aha, so that's what
they call our little poker party. Omega. Great! Do these
guys even know that in Greek it means "Great O"?

(b) The son of parents who served jail time for criminal syndicalism (union organizing).

(c) The son of a mother who raised money for Russian War Relief.

(d) The cousin of labor organizers Charles and Joseph (alias David) Persily.

(e) The "Mister Big" of West Coast Young Communists.

(f) A labor agitator who blew up two men with a hand grenade in an Arizona strike dispute.

(g) Observed lurking near UCLA's nuclear cyclotron used in the atomic bomb project.

(h) A known associate of underground and fugitive Communists. . . .

None of it is true except for b, c, d and h.

"MAKE IT EASY on us and yourself," Jeff advises. This is their MO. Arresting isn't their game, not unless it's a head-line-catching case, which we're not. They only want names which they probably already have on file but once you coop-erate they own you. It's an obligatory shaming ceremony. Do they get bonuses per name?

"Goodnight, Gracie," I politely shut the inner door on them.

Pause, then I hear them talking in low tones outside.

Mutt to Jeff, "Who's Gracie? Get a last name. Add her to his file."

Oh no, I've just ratted out America's favorite comedienne, Gracie Allen, George Burns's wife. Sorry, Gracie.

❖

THERE, THAT ISN'T so bad, is it? Except that after their visits I stumble into the bathroom and swallow antidiarrhea Paregoric because I've shit my pants. My hands blush purple and my spine bursts with so many pussy fearpimples I spend half the night rubbing Clearasil on myself. Some hero.

I pad back to bed and try to remember who is in it, Terry, but for the moment cannot recall my own name, much less hers.

PART THREE

16

First Day on the Job After My Lying Interview

And we'll never again ask a man to do anything that will poison his pride in himself or his work.

—William Holden as furniture factory manager McDonald Walling in *Executive Suite* (1954). Two of its stars, Jaffe clients Fredric March and Shelley Winters, are "graylisted."

S TILL IN THE mismatched jacket and pants that belong to Ray Kovacs, I'm hiding in my new second-floor office, its porthole window facing onto Sunset Boulevard, my name embossed on a plastic shield slid into a door groove for easy removal. As demanded by the new bosses, my formerly helmet-thick hair is cropped bristly to the skull, a style favored by the FBI, LA cops, and suburban dads in Bermuda shorts.

Every nerve end tells me to get out before I make a splendid mess of things. Unlike the William Morris and MCA agencies, Jaffe has no training program, no way to start from the bottom as a mailroom clerk; Sam and Mary expect a virgin agent to jump in and make deals from your first

day. Since my new office is the closest to Reception, I'm
also expected to deal with the Miss Lonelyhearts walk-ins
whom the other agents have no time for: fame-hungry wait-
resses, dentists, gas pump jockeys, and recent releases from
Camarillo State Hospital with this absolutely positively fabulous Academy Award script to sell. Unlike the other A-list
agencies, where unknowns have to jump through hoops just
to see an assistant's assistant secretary, Sam Jaffe insists on
an open-door policy "because you never know if you're
dealing with a crazy person or the next Gregory Peck or the
next Ben Hecht."

Just outside my door in the big office well are two strangers, my secretary "Addy with a y" and "Joanna," the receptionist who's told me that she is a rabbi's daughter and off
limits to wandering hands. All I know about Addy-with-a-y
is that she has astounding legs. She and Joanna throw me
reproving looks for practically cowering under my desk
instead of getting out there with the other agents to pound
pavement. And do what? What happens if I run into a college classmate who remembers me as a martyred campus
hero? It's happened already, at the Lighthouse jazz club,
when a girl from my class asked me what I was up to and
when I told her I could see her eyes flicker with disappoint-
ment. Hey pal, I couldn't pay the rent.

I roll down the Venetian blinds against the morning sun
blasting in from the Strip, and ignore a pile of unread scripts
on the desk to hunker down fetus-like in my Winchester
executive leather chair and study the agency's sacred Client
List and their "quotes":

CONFIDENTIAL—DO NOT REMOVE FROM OFFICE

What can I possibly do for these $1,000-a-week, $75,000-a picture-writers, directors, and star actors? On a good day in San Pedro I made $2 an hour. Until the work gave out, Jennie at her Catalina Swimwear knitting machine earned $70 a week.

The Client List should be sprinkled with sapphire dust. They're pieces of my life.

DONNA REED, the virginal hooker in *From Here to Eternity* . . . MARY ASTOR, my mom's favorite slut Brigid O'Shaughnessy, sent to the gallows by Bogart in *The Maltese Falcon* (*"You killed Miles and you're going over for it."*) . . . FREDRIC MARCH, hungrily embracing wife Myrna Loy after his return from war in *The Best Years of Our Lives* . . . JOSEPH COTTON, Orson Welles's best friend in *Citizen Kane* . . . JUDITH ANDERSON, mad lesbian Mrs. Danvers torching Manderley ablaze in *Rebecca* . . . VINCENT PRICE, demented artist mummifying his female victims in *House of Wax* . . . black-gloved killer JACK PALANCE in *Shane* . . .

DAVID NIVEN . . . RICHARD BURTON . . . GLORIA GRAHAME . . . ROD STEIGER . . . JOAN FONTAINE . . . GINGER ROGERS . . . RHONDA FLEMING . . . ERROL FLYNN . . . PETER LORRE . . . PAUL HENREID . . .

 . . . gods, sheer gods and goddesses.

❖

JESUITS SAY, "GIVE me a child for his first seven years and I'll give you the man." Exactly! I was lucky to have haunted movie houses in my most formative years, before the Catholic-enforced Production Code drove brazen sex from the screen. By the time the Code hacked films to pieces, my little boy's heart knew that real, real life existed only in the wild sexual craziness of Jean Harlow's iced-up pointy breasts, Joan Crawford's leer, Barbara Stanwyck's lowly file clerk cynically screwing her way up to the boss's penthouse. And, of course, was amazed and startled by the seductive anatomies of Busby Berkeley's chorus girls, whose close-up spread legs opened up a whole sexual issue for me long before I knew what sex was for. So the Catholics were right: I was ruined. Delightfully, permanently.

I look over the client list and my brain goes blank.

Mrs. Baker's tutorial boils down to a single sentence: "Get out there and lose your cherry with the neurotics and we'll gradually work you up to the psychopaths." In her dictionary, screenwriters are the neurotics; actors, the psychotics. Right off the bat I'm responsible for a golden list of screenwriters with Oscar-worthy credits like *Strangers on a Train, King Solomon's Mines, Winchester '73*, the Ginger Rogers–Fred Astaire spectacles, and my favorite lower-half-of-the-bill *Cult of the Cobra*. I nervously leaf through their unsold scripts on my desk, the ones I'm expected to sell, their polished competence reproaching me, story plots full of fast-paced action, eye-popping imagery, pulp magazine characters, one-line dialogue, brass-stapled into 120 pages. How am I expected to sell, sell, sell just from a typed list and a small mountain of brass-bound screenplays? I'm a cowboy on a horse plunging off a steep cliff into a raging torrent full of rocks and whirlpools. I must pick it up as I go along and fake it to buyers that I am on intimate terms with the clients. Apparently that's how the Jaffe system works for newbies. No wonder Mary Baker likes ex-servicemen used to jumping out of planes on the first try.

How can I minimize the harm I do to these people?

Duke, speak to me! Where is my inner John Wayne when I need him? I will not go out there in the midday sun to sell.

Pretending a bathroom break, I sneak down the circular iron stairs, out a side alley, and flee across Sunset traffic to the Cock 'n Bull for a bracer where Romeo, the Russian émigré barman, tells me I'm crazy to walk out on a new career. He risked his life to desert from the Red Army, so what's my problem? "*Baytsim,*" he growls leaning across the bar confidentially, "where are your balls?" Yes, where?

Slinking back in the office, I push past Addy-with-a-y who follows on her Ziegfeld legs, draws up a chair, and flips open her spiral shorthand notebook, pencil poised.

We stare at each other.

She shuts the notebook and recrosses those legs. She's, what?, ten or fifteen years older than the other secretaries, works at the peroxide and L'Oréal anti-wrinkle cream, very short skirts and big-time makeup.

"Oh, you poor child," she shakes her head. "You don't have a clue, do you?"

Briskly, motherly, she scrawls on her notepad an inter-office memo listing all the client calls and studio visits I've made this day which she'll wait to circulate until evening. "And you will do them," she adds. "Don't make a liar of both of us."

And that's how I get through the first day.

I actually drive out to Warner Brothers, Universal, and Republic, but have no idea how to proceed, so retreat in a fluster to the Jaffe office without knocking on a single door. "How did it go, sweetie?" Addy asks on my exhausted return.

I confess that once inside studio gates I mainly hid in my car. I don't even know what I'm supposed to be selling.

She smiles wonderfully: "Selling? Why, yourself, of course."

She leaves, then pops her head back in.

"Wait and see, tomorrow will be better."

Actually tonight is better. When most everyone has gone, Addy slips into my office and discreetly shuts the door.

I look up.

She says, "I'm a single mother and my son plays the trombone in the school band and he gets failing grades and drinks Virginia Dare wine. He's all I ever worry about. Do you want to get this done and over with now? Clients soon will take up most of your time and you won't need the distraction of thinking 'Will she, won't she?'"

She reads my mind like my mother.

We do it in the back storeroom stacked with mimeo paper and boxes of stationery. From behind a shelf she drags a futon—who else uses it?—and spreads it on the floor after locking the door and switching off the light by pulling a string on the overhead bulb. I do what I'm told, and it's great. Afterwards, she puts on her clothes and says, "See? Feel better? As the soap ads say, 'No mess no clutter.'"

And she's right.

17

Where the Bodies Are Buried in Hollywood

L ABOR TROUBLES ARE the movie industry's clos- eted ghost. Film studios have always preferred to bribe gangster goons in exchange for worker peace. The current blacklist is an anti-union strategy. What begins as a minor jurisdictional spat between the crooked union, International Alliance of Theatrical Stage Employees (IATSE), and its smaller cleaner rival, the Conference of Studio Unions (CSU), explodes in picket line violence with blood, tear gas, and cracked heads at the Warner Brothers gate. Jack Warner will never forgive his employees who picketed.

The defeat of CSU breaks labor power—and the pro- gressive movement—in Hollywood. Thousands of men and women, many of whom have spent their lives in studio jobs, are fired and hundreds of strikers are jailed and tried in front of judges so prejudiced that juries set them free.

Those employees—electricians, sound editors, story ana- lysts, etc.—who survive the broken strike are scared of being known as malcontents and, God forbid, Communists. At the Jaffe agency, Zack Silver and Mary Baker's assistant Cricket Kendall are among former jailed strikers who got their fingers burned. They haven't "sold out," just aren't looking for more trouble.

The former New Deal liberal, Ronald Reagan, Screen Actors Guild president, who is also FBI informant "T-10," has learned his lesson, too. Using his union position, he signs a secret waiver exempting our competitor Lew Wasserman's Music Corporation of America from a federal law that forbids agents from also engaging in film production. Through this maneuver MCA is the only such agency granted favored monopoly status, which gives Wasserman a big advantage over rivals like Sam Jaffe. In exchange for this favor, MCA makes Reagan a part owner of its TV company and a very rich man.

18

Act of Violence

F RESH ON THE job I'm anxious to impress.

Not all of my working clients, who I get up the nerve to visit, are overjoyed to have a junior agent foisted on them. Some see it as a sign of the agency's melancholy estimate of their profit potential. Must set this straight. Somehow.

Meanwhile, Mary Baker is trying to smooth out my rough edges by inviting me into business meetings with stellar clients. In her office Donna Reed's husband-manager Tony Owen lays out his discontent, "Enough already with Donna's sweetheart of Sigma Chi roles. Find me a story where in this first scene the guy walks in and slaps the shit out of her . . . we gotta shake up her audience!" Owen may talk tough about Donna's movie future, but from industry gossip I know they're looking for career insurance by planning a TV show and are discreetly sending out the word to hire blacklisted writers, God bless them. Off in a corner of Mary's office, Anita, the secretary who first told me about the job, is taking notes when accidentally her handbag falls open and the contents tumble out on Mary's Persian carpet, revealing Anita's diaphragm. Being in a round disc case, it rolls around and around interminably while all of us watch transfixed, until Anita falls on her knees to grab the gyrating object only to watch in horror as a second diaphragm rolls from her bag. Anita bursts into embarrassed tears. But Donna, bless her Iowa heart, simply breaks the tension by also getting down on her knees alongside Anita and cracking, "Is that what they call a sex toy? My Tony Junior, he's only four, but would love playing with it." How could you not love a client like Donna Reed?

❖

BY WATCHING HOW other agents operate, eavesdropping on their phone calls, keeping an ear open to office gossip, and copying Mary Baker's tonal mix of flinty and intimate, I get the hang of it. Agenting really isn't so different from union or community organizing. ("YOU FUCKING LYING SCUM GET THE FUCK OUT OF MY OFFICE WITH YOUR SCHMATTE!") It all has to do with "presentation of self," that is, being an actor. Addy is right, you're selling not your product but who you are, your personality, and who I am now isn't Mitchum or Cagney or Gable but me. Whoever he is at any given moment.

But always guided by Mary Baker's instructions:

(a) "Go to parties, openings, screenings, bar mitzvahs. Show up even when you're not invited, they won't know the difference."

(b) "When negotiating, ask for double and settle for half. Be ready to lose the job. Say 'Sorry we can't do business.' Then exit, look at your watch, stall for five minutes, call back and tell them your client has agreed over your strong protest. They'll know you're lying but so what?"

(c) "Perform. Agents are great actors. Better even than the clients. You become the role you're rehearsing. Your Academy Award is the Christmas bonus."

(d) "Feel sincere. Be sincere. Fake it if you don't feel it. Don't worry, if you fake it long enough you'll feel it."

(e) "Finally, scare the buyer as well as your clients. Make them worry, in the backs of their tiny little minds, that you can beat them up. Make them be afraid of you. Just a little."

The last part sticks in my mind. Ray would love it.

I do what comes naturally or what Ray would do in my shoes when the jungle telegraph crackles that a rival William Morris agent is flirting with, on the verge of stealing, one of my always-in-work clients, "Walter Isaacs," at Warner Brothers on a $500-a-week contract. I track down the WMA agent at Villa Nova on Sunset across from Scandia just down from George Cukor's house.

"Sandy Weinberg," the thief, is feeding his soul at the bar with bourbon shots when I walk in from the sunny street before the dinner crowd. He looks up in surprise when I take the stool next to his.

"Hi ya, Sandy."

"I know you?"

"Clancy Sigal. With the Jaffe office."

"Oh yeah."

Back to his booze.

We sit there hunched over our drinks.

I start, "Walter Isaacs."

No response.

Sandy, evasively: "He's a friend of mine."

I hook my foot around a leg of his stool and pull hard. Over he goes, ass over end, sprawled on the floor.

"Get a new friend," I say and walk out.

The next morning Mary and Sam are furious. In Sam's office:

"Are you nuts?" Mary demands. But she looks at me with new respect.

Me, protesting: "But he stole a client."

Sam: "Yes? And so?"

Mary: "Right this minute go and personally apologize to Sandy."

"For what? He did the crime."

Mary: "Since when is kidnapping another agent's client a crime? It's normal business. You can't go around actually beating up people who poach. We all steal."

Sam: "Tell him you were drunk."

Me: "He knows I wasn't."

Mary: "He'll appreciate the lie."

Me: "I'm not going to apologize. Walter Isaacs is my client."

Sam sighs, "Since when? Walter Isaacs is everybody's client. Know how many times he's left us?"

Rehearsing contrite, I drive to the Beverly Hills office of William Morris, and Sandy Weinberg makes me sweat waiting for an hour by his receptionist's desk. Then he leans back in his leather chair just like mine and listens carefully to my apology and lets my words hang in the air so we can both study the hypocrisy as he ponders a response.

His first words, "You'd break my leg for a cheap piece of shit like Walter Isaacs? Man, where are your priorities?"

On my way out of the Morris office I ask his secretary would she kindly get me a cup of water, and when she's gone I riffle through her desk until I find it:

CONFIDENTIAL—DO NOT LET OUT OF THIS OFFICE

A list of Sandy's clients.

When I proudly report back to Sam and Mary that after apologizing I stole Sandy's client list and have identified some "vulnerables," Sam says, "Now you get it. That's our boy."

At Warners the next day I drop in on Walter Isaacs in his writer's office as he's pounding the keys on a Cold War spy script. He looks up from the typewriter.

"Walter, I hear Sandy Weinberg is romancing you."

He looks up from the typewriter. "Are you going to hit me?"

Good. The word is out.

19

Socrates in Tasseled Loafers

AFTER I TANGLE with Sandy at La Rue's, word spreads through Jaffe that I might be a keeper. The imprimatur comes in the form of veteran agents—"Zack Silver," "Jonathan Buck," and "Ace Kantor"—taking me under their wing.

Zack (Navy, minesweeper, Atlantic), affable and almost supernaturally laid back—the office nice guy—is the in-house classics scholar, an outdoorsman who hunts with rifle, knife, crossbow, and is married to a Native American woman with fishing rights on the Puyallup River. Jonny Buck (Colonial Club, Princeton) is mandated to teach me negatives like how not to tread on other agents' turf, how not to take producers' insults personally, how not to make a clumsy visual presentation of myself, above all how not to be a pain in the ass to Jonny himself. He is a bare-faced anti-Semite. ("You went to school where? JEWCLA? That explains it.") Ace Kantor (Marines, Pacific), former tennis semi-pro, deals hyper-smoothly with marquee-brand actors and directors. Through Ace I will meet-and-greet most of Jaffe's A-list actors. He is life-greedy, avaricious, collegial, and extraordinarily handsome in the George Hamilton style.

Each senior agent will waste a day on me.

"No matter what you hear, this is an honest business. Crooks don't last long. Short-term you can screw somebody on a deal but the word gets out that you're untrustworthy. In the long run it doesn't pay off. And it's the payoff that counts." —Zack Silver

"Right away the executives I deal with at Metro and Fox will mistake you for the mail boy. Look how you're dressed! Schmatte-ville. Padded shoulders! If you're not prepared to invest in a Brooks Brothers suit, wool: no synthetic drek like Dacron, narrow shoulders, three-inch lapels, get out of the business. I'll send you to my tailor. Genial works—look at Zack—but arrogance is better—look at me. They respect anyone who looks down on them. Don't worry, you'll figure out your own style . . . God help us." —Jonathan Buck

"Go silent, go stealthy, don't draw fire. Smile even if they're throwing bricks at you. Be careful where you laugh. Show respect even to toads. These are very insecure men you're dealing with. You have the goods, they have the money, it's only haggling, goes back to the Egyptians, I'll sell you my camel for your daughter. Trust is everything. Lose a deal rather than lose their

*trust in you. It's okay to lie to your clients about pos-
sibilities because nobody likes bad news. Keep hope
alive. Remember: never bury a client just because they
look dead. You're Doctor Frankenstein, your job is to
bring the monster back to life with your personal magne-
tism. If they change agents after you make them rich, it
doesn't mean they're ungrateful, just Hollywood humans
in a jungle on fire. You don't play tennis? Pity. You lift
weights? Honey, this ain't Muscle Beach."* —Ace Kantor

❖

FOR A RAW recruit like me the San Fernando Valley studios—Universal, Warners and Republic—are a boot camp
to make my mistakes. As the newest agent I'm also assigned
extra shit work, going in cold at sub–Poverty Row out-
lets like Monogram and its sister Allied Artists and Eagle-
Lion and any dinky offices located in the grubby end of
Hollywood where fly-by-night producers hang their shingle
by the week and pay fifty bucks a script if the writer is lucky.
The agent I replaced, "Flip Edwards" (née Feivel Eisenberg),
sallow, smelling of Old Kentucky, unshaven, rumpled suit,
aggressively depressed—a dramatic contrast to the rest of
us—has been exiled to the industry's Siberia, in the shadow
of Bekins-type concrete warehouses in parts of Hollywood
no star would be seen dead in, because Sam and Mary don't
have the heart to fire their only employee who publicly suffers from war nerves eight years after his war is over. He's
the only agent to wear in his lapel the tiny brass insignia GIs
call the ruptured duck to indicate honorable discharge.

"See these teeth, New Boots," Flip counsels me in a grubby little diner. "In the squad they called me The Smiler. Face in the shit under an 88 barrage hey I'm still laughing. Ever been under a tree burst? We told replacements like you to walk point in the Ardennes why get used to their names. You never even made it across? (Long sigh) Well, you walk point now. Don't bother to knock, walk right in and keep smiling and *talk* them stories don't leave them anything to *read* most of them never got past the third grade. I love it down here. Nobody's buckin' for promotion. End of the line, New Boots."

EACH JAFFE AGENT cultivates a "selling" voice, a form of ventriloquism. We're actors reciting lines from a script depending on whether delivering good or bad news, or if we're inebriated (often), or to intimidate. Just the way you pick up the phone is a self portrait. ("Clancy here—kill for the sake of killing! Who's this?") Walking through the office in the early evening as agents roll up client calls is like listening to fourteen radio dramas at once.

Whenever I'm through with this job, I wonder if Orson Welles might hire me for his Mercury Theatre on the Air to play any role required.

20

Gangster Chic

MARY BAKER IS a fashion Führer. "Goddamit, Clancy, are those argyle socks? Give me a break, you're not a campus cutie any more!" Meaning, it's time to toss Ray's throwaways and Dress For Success.

A few streets up from the office, at 8804 Sunset where it curves away from West Hollywood, Jaffe has an arrangement with the gangster-haberdasher-and-florist-as-a-front Mickey Cohen, armed robber, killer-to-order: and Ben Siegel's bodyguard until Jack Dragna or Meyer Lansky had Bugsy's face shot off on Linden Drive just around the corner from Mary Baker's mansion. For show and cover, Mickey operates, among other legit businesses, a men's clothing store on the Strip. Even though it exposes him to drive-by assassination, Cohen is a publicity hog who enjoys loitering outside his shop waving to passing tourists. A starfucker, he extends discounts to Jaffe agents in return for access to premieres and parties where he and his bodyguards can mix with movie stars.

Mrs. Baker doesn't trust me to shop alone so one morning sends her two enforcers, my mentors Zack Silver and Jonny Buck, into Mickey's shop to supervise a makeover. At the front door, as in a Grade-B film, a toothpick-chewing bodyguard in an open-necked yellow silk shirt and immaculately pressed trousers eye-frisks us before he lets us in to meet the man himself. Meyer Harris Cohen emerges from behind a wheeled rack of jackets and empty hangers, Mickey in a double-wide-shouldered off-white gabardine suit and his trademark custom-made Joy Lord Hatter of New York fedora, all vain muscle and five o'clock shadow. He's on his way to a four-year prison stretch, but you'd never know it from his demeanor.

Without a word to Zack and Jonny, like a real bespoke tailor, Mickey circles as if I'm a boxer in the ring with him. Pug-busted nose, serious bowlegs, formidable jowls, he sets himself like the featherweight pro fighter that he was—against pretty good opponents I'm told.

"So," he rumbles to style-maven Jonny, "Ivy League or *proster chamoole*?" What's that? I ask. Zack says, "Basically low-class shithead."

Must establish my personal credibility with LA's most notorious crook.

"Mr. Cohen, I ran numbers after school for Max Glauber the bookie." Quick as a flash Mickey responds, "Yeah? You lie." I go, "Cigar store. Roosevelt Road by Homan." Real Chicagoans always say 'by,' not at or near. Jonny and Zack look at me in surprise. Cohen appraises me a long moment, then smiles broadly. We're bonded in Chicago graft.

"Come," he gestures me into the back room, "and you guys jerk off a while."

An hour later I emerge splendiferous in a three-button double-breasted pinstriped Brooks Brothers-style suit, a handmade tie with mother-of-pearl tie bar, a diamond-design white silk shirt, and penny loafer oxblood shoes— some of the clothes labeled, some not, all obviously having fallen off the back of a truck, while in a box under my arm I carry a single-breasted two-button glen plaid Savile Row ensemble plus cardigan ("Cary Grant loves that slim Continental style," gushes Mickey), all to match under his careful eye. In the full-length mirror I look like a mafia lawyer. Zack and Jonny simply stare.

His arm around me, Mickey walks me out of the store and wishes me all the luck in the world.

He bestows upon me a classic Chicago benediction. He says, "Kid, go out there and kill 'em."

Leaving Mickey's establishment in a new suit, shirt, tie, and even shoes, makes me feel a thousand percent different. A new man. A company guy. The mask fits.

21

Ghost Story

WORD OF THE new boy's willingness to battle for clients also reaches the actors as well as writers.

"What's that I hear? You beating up people for Mister Jaffe? THEN WHY DON'T YOU DO IT FOR ME, *FAULER SACK!*"

My Blitz German tells me client Peter Lorre is calling me a lazy shit.

Peter Lorre (who has become a friend) and I lunch frequently, commiserating with each other. We like each other for our faults. My pain is hard to locate, his very specific: typecasting.

Peter is multi-masked like me, but the similarity ends there. He's a product of pre-Hitler Europe's dense cosmopolitan culture, working with Bertolt Brecht and Kurt Weill, and is part of Hollywood's large colony of anti-fascist exiles so many of whom—*aber natürlich!*—play movie Nazis. His idea of light reading, as I found on visiting his Hollywood Hills home, is Goethe, Schiller, Rilke, and Heine. That's one mask. Then there's the much-too-remembered pedophile in Fritz Lang's German-language *M* that made him world-famous but also forever trapped as an employable ghoul. And then there's the "real" Peter Lorre, a glum fat man hooked on cocaine and morphine from a gallbladder infection and which he abuses to ease himself over the discomfort of wearing all those sharp-edged masks that claw at his plumpish, self-mocking, always troubled face. Finally, he's a proud first-time father in his fifties who swings wildly from self-deprecating hilarity to suicidal gloom.

He sums up his constant psychic or physical discomfort as "Berlin yesterday, Los Angeles today." Like some other Jaffe clients he got out of Germany in time, fleeing to Paris, London, and finally Hollywood. He confides, "It's stupid, *blödsinnig*, isn't it? This McCarthy business . . . this Rosenberg business . . . all waiting for a Reichstag fire to give them the excuse." Peter takes personally the open anti-Semitism of the House Committee whose members single out witnesses by their foreign-sounding names. Lorre says, "Wait till they get to Ladislav Löwenstein."

My mistake is confessing to him that I failed to shoot Hermann Goering at the Nuremberg war crimes trial where I'd slipped in with a .45 under my khaki shirt. That's when Peter reaches across the restaurant table to tap my head, hard. "You were there and did nozzing! *Schwachkopf!*" He sighs. "Idiot! No wonder you get me only these crazy parts. Now they want me to go to the Congo and who knows? Play a cannibal? If only you knew how I hate bugs and ants and even grass!" Without pausing for breath, "You noodle, why didn't you shoot?"

Our lunch table talk usually gets around to the bizarre roles we find him. "Always the monster," he wails, "not even a normal monster." (For eight films he even played the Japanese Buddhist detective *Mr. Moto.*) Full of despair and self-loathing one day at the Brown Derby, he finally snaps over a Sachertorte and leaps from his chair to wander among the startled guests, being "Peter Lorre" the *beast with five fingers*, his chubby upraised hands like claws, his teeth bared in an agonizing smile. He sidles among the tables leering at a seated woman, hissing "I could murder you with love, my dear."

Desperate to provoke a reaction from an affectless Hollywood crowd, Peter deliberately crashes into tables, screaming at individuals, "*You . . . you bungled it . . . You . . . you imbecile. You bloated idiot* (to an obese man) . . . *you stupid fathead . . .*" and drops to his knees in front of them all, sobbing his lines as Joel Cairo to Sidney Greenstreet in *The Maltese Falcon.*

Utter silence in the Brown Derby; even the waiters are mesmerized.

Then Peter gets to his feet, brushes off his trousers, and makes a low bow amidst a spatter of applause and nervous laughter.

"See?" he accuses me. "They don't want me. They want him."

Trouble is, I want him, too. Him is my living.

Peter reads my eyes. "Et tu, Clancy?" he says simply.

22

The Thousand Guns
of Dale and Peter

MY CLIENT, COWBOY star Dale Robertson, is the anti–Peter Lorre; a former boxer, wounded vet (tanks, Silver and Bronze Stars), champion rodeo rider, and Indian-fighter in *Sitting Bull* and a string of unremarkable but marketable westerns. Unlike five-foot-five, out-of-shape Ladislav Löwenstein, six-foot-yay-tall, good-natured, loping-easy Dale in his buckskin jacket and Oklahoma boots and Boss of the Plains Stetson is a genuine ranch-hand hero, what John Wayne ought to be. Dale doesn't drink, smoke, chew, or swear beyond "darn" and "shucks." He is that strange Hollywood animal: He is what he seems.

My friendship with Dale is rooted in a mutual love of the old cowboy movies we both grew up on. What? You don't know Art Accord or Tumbleweed Baker? And also my respect for what he started out as, a horse wrangler hanging around Poverty Row back lots waiting for a $5-a-day job as an extra. In a Ships diner down the Strip we've spent hours over coffee and pie hammering out an original western script, "The Thousand Guns of Justin Malloy," a simple clean story. Peter Lorre is hungry to play a non-ghoul, and Dale and Peter are so mismatched it's perfect.

Most surprising is that when I bring the Oklahoma cowboy and Viennese intellectual together in my office, it's love at first sight. What they don't love is how I've revamped Dale's original story to exploit the current market trends; my version has it all, a coward-turned-hero sheriff, a mysterious foreign doctor delivering a baby on Christmas Eve to a redeemed dance-hall floozy, even a ticking clock like *High Noon*.

I will co-executive-produce the movie.

Dale and Peter listen in respectful silence in my office as I read my rewrite to them. Both actors ask for time to think it over and go off to have a drink, a ginger ale in Dale's case. An hour later, that same afternoon, they return, in a good mood.

Dale drawls for them. "Clancy, we love you to death. We thought you were different from the other agents, but you've turned my idea into crap. What's got into you, son?"

I'm shocked.

Peter chimes in, "My friend, it's shit. Why are you bending over backward to kiss your ass to succeed in this business?"

Dale comes around my desk to give me a manly hug.

"You're still young, Clancy." Meaning, my fingers definitely do not dance along the typewriter keys to find the right "story arc."

Peter jumps from his chair and stands with his chubby legs wide apart and pretends to hold two Colt six-guns on me pointing at my heart.

He puts on a drawl like Dale's.

"Better git out of my town pronto, pardner. Or your life won't be worth a plugged nickel."

What is Peter telling me?

❖

IT'S AN OPEN secret in the office that I will physically intervene if a client (and his commission) are in jeopardy. I kibitz on their screenplays, confront rival agents in studio commissaries, and swipe movie material off studio story editors' desks to sneak to unemployed clients. *You do what you must.*

23

The Big Knife

H ERE'S WHAT I do: am on call twenty-four hours a
day to drum up jobs and a paycheck for any of the
sixty-four men and a few women writers for whom I share
responsibility; honey-talk and scout roles for our unemployed actors; pitch the Jaffe product in restaurant urinals
and at bar mitzvahs; and steal humans from rival agencies
while shielding my own from predatory raids.

But most ardently, as my position at Jaffe becomes more
secure, I can afford to indulge my passion for the mutts, the
hard sells, the odd writer with the freakiest talent: Nelson
Algren, Horace McCoy, John Fante, James Agee, an honor
roll of novelists and poets who have a calling, not a movie
career, and really don't belong in Hollywood, but as long as
they're here, I'm here.

With the big, expensive, always-in-demand screenwriters—"calls in" not "calls out"—all I have to do is sit back
and collect their commissions: Ernie Lehman, Frank Nugent,
Danny Fuchs, Charlie Lederer, Frank Davis—craftsmen

who never took a screenwriting class but have imaginations born of colorful, grown-up lives as club bouncers, pipe layers, truck drivers, and combat pilots.

The myth is, they come for the money and stay for the palm trees, which is how Hollywood corrupts them. Is it true? What about slum-bred Daniel Fuchs whom we now keep working at $1,250 a week when an average Ohio factory guy with overtime can make, if he's lucky, a hundred bucks? Far from feeling guilt, Dan seems blissfully at home with his family in sunny Southern Cal.

For the moment, dismiss the strange case of dramatist Clifford Odets who is having a happy hour selling his screenplays for top dollar while collecting Impressionist art and having his pick of beautiful women like King Kong's squeeze, gorgeous Fay Wray, around his Hollywood Hills swimming pool. Last year, after one of my serial blacklistings I had nothing better to do than hitch across the country to help set up chairs at a New York lecture hall for an anti-blacklist rally where Odets was the inspired and inspirational speaker imploring the overflow crowd to "Resist! Resist! Now or never! On your feet or on your knees—the decision is yours!" The crowd, including me standing on a chair and whistling and clapping, responded with a great roar, as it had done almost twenty years before on the first night of his stirring play, *Waiting for Lefty,* which climaxed with the taxi driver hero exhorting the audience to "Strike, strike!" And then, the very next morning after the blacklist rally, guided by advice from his Group Theatre comrade Elia Kazan (the man who had previously named him to the red hunters), who had sought advice from his shrink, he gave up names to a congressional committee. What possesses men like Kazan and Odets?

Yet the sad truth is, betraying their friends had liberated each of these artists to do some of their finest work.

Might my creative future, like Odets's, lie in ruining **nine names**?

Mary Baker calls me in.

She sips from a Bloody Mary. At 9:30 A.M.

Problem. She's had complaints that I'm ignoring the expensive clients for my mutts who, yes, privately, I regard as too good for movie work. "What, you're God? *Vei is mir.* Who are you to make life and death judgments? What future do you offer our formerly dirt poor but now rich clients, they should go back sleeping three in a bed in the Bronx with cockroaches? Asthma, rickets, TB, toilet down the hall?" She swallows her drink. "Get outta here and do your job!"

Chastened, I skulk out. She's right, my responsibility is to service clients without prejudgment. "Selling out" only if I fail to do it conscientiously. So what if they use the money I earn them to retile a swimming pool or send their kids to snooty schools like Buckley or Chadwick. Mary is right, I'm not God.

So this afternoon, I'm patrolling along the off-white corridors of Burbank's Warner Brothers writers' building, hung with life-sized photos of the star stable (Bette Davis, Bogart, Cagney), no longer shy, making courtesy calls on my client list, "*Hello. How are you? Any problems? No? That's good, glad to see ya . . .*" when I pass by Walter Isaacs's cubicle.

Walter is a competent $500-a-week contract writer (I made the deal) on whom we collect commission week in week out, rain or shine: the best kind of client.

He looks up from his typewriter to greet me gloomily, "*A broche!*"

Sorry to hear it, I say. Trouble?

Walter is sweating to meet a five o'clock deadline for a third-act climax to the Cold War espionage script he's been assigned or else his goose is cooked, contract canceled.

Walter is the popular idea of a screenwriter, unkempt with anxiety, pudgy and bespectacled with big wet eyes, will write anything for hire since his pulp magazine days, miserable and glossy with perspiration as always.

"Hmmm, I see," says Dr. Sigal, not wanting to lose Walter's steady commission. It's easy to poke holes at someone else's script and then fill the holes. Sometimes, on the q.t., clients in script trouble come by my place, and I charge a couple of hundred bucks for a repair job. But with only an hour to go, this is no time for haggling.

He sits me down and confesses that all his drafts have been rejected by director Michael Curtiz and by the head honcho himself, Jack Warner, who refuses to let the project, a Green or Red Beret foolishness, go forward until he knows how it ends. Micromanaging from the top is unusual. Most screenwriters are hired mechanics on a script-factory production line who never get to meet the director or producer, let alone studio head. The writer is expected to churn out pages fed into a machine which spits them out as a shooting script which a director, if lucky, has a weekend to read just before commencement of principal photography. But Walter's story demands extra-special treatment because there's a "political" angle.

Walter himself pretends to no politics except for the normal Hollywood liberalism which means he'll take any job no matter how racist or reactionary while making an annual tax-deductible contribution to the ACLU. But, he says, there's a "delicate problem" on this piece of *chazerai*. Because in bygone years the studio made an anti-Nazi movie or two and featured working-class heroes, the brothers Jack and Harry Warner, especially Jack, despite his wealth and power, are terrified that in the current purge climate they will be painted as treasonous Jews. Jack is so nervous that his wartime madly pro-Russian *Mission to Moscow* (a box-office dog) will be held against him that he almost broke an ankle running to Washington to denounce his suspect (i.e., liberal) writers and actors, especially those who picketed in the big Warner Brothers strike. And that ace of all cinematic trades, Mike Curtiz, Walter Isaacs's current director, who helmed *Mission to Moscow,* is so jittery that he's demanding an insanely patriotic Stars-and-Stripes-Forever climax to Walter's otherwise routine script.

Poor Walter is constipated. Blocked. Gosh, do I ever identify.

Like a priest in the confessional, I lean my head almost touching Walter's as he outlines the plot of "Naples Nocturne" from an *Argosy* pulp magazine story I sold. See, our hero, this handsome Italian-American mobster, secretly is released from Alcatraz by submarine as a US counterspy assigned to his family's native Italy to eliminate a Russian spy ring. Once landed off Naples, he gets involved with a beautiful Communist spy; the studio has cast this new girl, Sophia Loren. "It's pishposh hugger mugger," Walter sighs. "Murders, dark alleys, I've done a million of them . . . the point is, my guy Vinnie needs to die a huge American patriot at the end." He looks pleadingly at me. "It just won't come."

"Is that all?" I push my chair back.

He stares at me in dubious hope.

"You write?" he asks his kid agent.

"Disappear, Walter. Give me an hour."

"But," glancing at the wall clock, "it's already four o'clock."

"I'm a fast typist." I shoo him out of his own office. Every week rain or shine the agency collects ten percent of Walter's check which goes into my bonus.

At 4:45 Walter reappears, looking grim and frantic.

I hand him pages including carbon copies.

"Walter," I patiently explain, "here it is. Vinnie is an ex-Marine. In Korea he caught shrapnel in his head as he's leading a charge against the hordes of Red Chinese yelling '*banzai*!'—"

Walter interrupts. "Only the Japs do *banzai*, buddy. I was on Guadalcanal. I don't know what the hell the Chinese do."

"—don't worry about it. 'Die Yankee Dog!', whatever. And he's got this head wound that turned him into a mad dog killer but it's really a frame-up we don't show till the last reel. The same plot you used in *Man of the Gun*, remember?

Anyway, when the American government sends him to fight the Soviet rats in Italy—you're not going on location, are you? All back projection, right?—the Communists murder him after he rescues the spy girl who has recanted and there's this death scene in the church, then bam! Bam! These commie bastards have no respect for the Pope or human dignity, and in the very last shot they're about to bury Vinnie in his grandfather's simple country graveyard at the foot of Mount Etna, no wait, that's in Sicily, make it Vesuvius, with smoke belching to make it more dramatic, and when they bury him the big reveal is, guess what? Around his neck under his shirt he has a Distinguished Service Cross for gallantry in battle . . ."

Walter stares at me in a kind of horror. "Jesus, that's shit. It's beautiful. I'll have to tweak it because you can't kill off the leading man, it's a studio rule, depresses the audience. But you got it!"

A few weeks later, I drop in on Walter Isaacs at Warners. "Howzit going, paisan?"

He looks up with spaniel eyes. "You mean, did they buy it?"

He sighs again, deeply. "They put another writer on because my new end is so good they hiked the budget, so now that it's an 'A' picture they need the insurance of a writer with an Academy Award. But no hurt feelings, they raised me to $750."

"We won," I say.

"You're fired as my agent," Walter says.

"What?"

"If I can get raises without asking, why do I need you? Anyway, I'm at a different level now. Lew Wasserman over at MCA just signed me."

I sputter, "But I wrote that fucking end. You need me!"

He looks at me very calmly.

"I wrote the end," he says.

I look deep into Walter's eyes.

Yes. He truly believes it.

❖

"THAT *MOMSER* WALTER," Mary laughs about his defection. "He's already fired us, what? five, six times. But you have a personal relationship with him and that's what he'll remember when MCA screws him, which they will, and he comes back to us." She pauses. "But make him crawl a little."

Personal relationships is the ticket to ride.

Except that my most personal relationship is with my near-brother Ray Kovacs.

24

The Trial of the Century

Greta Garbo (as fanatic Russian Communist Nina Ivanova Yakushova): We don't have men like you in my country.

Melvyn Douglas (as her Paris bourgeois boyfriend Count Leon): Thank you.

Greta Garbo: That is why I believe in the future of my country.

—From *Ninotchka* (1939)

B Y RIGHTS, RADOVAN Kovacs shouldn't even be a paid-up Communist because—true story—he lost his older brother Andy in a Stalinist prison camp after Andy volunteered to "help build socialism" in Russia but was trapped in the Soviet spy madness. Their mother, a founding member of the Croatian Communist branch, hasn't heard from her oldest son for years despite weekly trips by Greyhound bus to picket the Soviet consulate in San Francisco. But Ray and his mom refuse to quit the Party out of dumb loyalty or sheer cussedness.

Emotionally Ray and I are twins, hip-joined by blithe ignorance of not knowing what we want to do with our lives, and by the dope we take (him cocaine, me Walgreens pharmacy-by-prescription), and a mutual contempt for left-wing victimology clichés like "persecuted" and "harassed." We've partied together, jinked in the open skies in his Piper Cub, been in the same jail cell, and slept side by side in the same bed or on the same floor. His girl Terry, who is now mine, is something else to share. Ray and I take it out on each other, wrestling and punching demons rather than hit others, which we do, too.

❖

IT ENDS BADLY for him.

The one night I turn Ray loose because I'm at a sneak pre-view (*Singin' in the Rain*) with our client Donald O'Connor, Ray goes to some flea-bitten bop bar on Vermont, picks up Chachi Lopez, an East-side amateur hooker, a high school dropout with a Veronica Lake peek-a-boo peroxide blonde hairdo and a sturdy body to match his. They date, and then—oh shock horror for our bachelor days!—fly off in a rented plane to marry in Yuma. Good Marxist Ray "educates" her; and practically overnight she flips over into Chachi Super-Red, a jargon-spouting 100-percenter. A few months lapse when I don't see Ray and then he calls dispirited because his new wife, now a loyal Party member, has brought him up on charges of male supremacy, white chauvinism, "infantile leftism," and "right deviationism," to name only a few. As paranoid as the FBI, the Party defies the witch hunt by conducting its own purge . . . of Ray.

There will be a trial, and he wants me as defense counsel. He must be kidding.

❖

SCENE: A TRACT house in Panorama City in a valley cul-de-sac, shades drawn in the makeshift courtroom in a small stifling front parlor where on a plastic sheet-covered couch four Party members—a white man, a white woman, an African American man, and an Asian American woman, ethnic bases covered—are the jury of Ray's peers. I've seen them around, an aeronautics engineer, high school teacher, music store clerk, and Party bureaucrat, respectively. The principal accuser is Ray's wife Chachi, who has slimmed down and actually is quite fetching in her rolltop jeans and Pendleton shirt.

The trial lasts until dawn.

Chachi is a surprisingly effective prosecutor. Her evidence piles up starting with Ray's original crime of picking her up in a bar. "That's male chauvinism right there." She then launches into a summing-up speech that is, frankly, magnificent. Here is this Boyle Heights girl, who when Ray first met her was a toilet-mouthed *chola* who probably hadn't opened a book in her life, now holding the floor pounding away at her husband for, among other things, demeaning her by giving her books to read "and telling me what to think as if I don't have a brain."

She turns on Ray. "He did not make me who I am today. I made myself!"

Ray stares at her admiringly.

In a bathroom break I advise him to plead *nolo contendere*, no contest, and walk away with a fuck-you, but he's perversely proud of Chachi. "Isn't she great? And anyway, submitting to Party discipline might help me get my head together and put me back on track. Just speak up for me, that's all."

Jesus, I say, that Nazi ack-ack must have shredded your brains.

He sighs as he goes back in, "That it did."

My rising to Ray's defense is a kiss of death because in their circles I'm known as a "friendly drop," to be handled with tongs.

Around sunup the verdict comes in. What a surprise, guilty as charged. Sentence: expulsion. Well, at least it's not a bullet in the nape of the neck.

On the drive back to LA I say, "Well, you sonofabitch, you sure kicked the shit out of yourself tonight."

He stares ahead in the glare of passing headlights.

"It's all good," he keeps repeating. "All good."

❖

AFTER THE POISONED air at Ray's "trial" the harsh hustling atmosphere at the Jaffe Agency breathes sweet as honeysuckle. I get an almost sexual charge in whistling up a job for a client—a writing or acting assignment, sometimes even a whole movie "project"—out of nothing but spit and desire. If I can't write at least I can do the next best thing, deceive.

25

Sweet Smell of Success

Burt Lancaster (as unscrupulous columnist J.J. Hunsecker: My right hand hasn't seen my left hand in thirty years.

—From *Sweet Smell of Success* (1957) by Jaffe client Ernest Lehman and Clifford Odets

R OD STEIGER IS another problem. This young rising actor has been profitable to the house, but after scoring as Brando's gangster brother in *On the Waterfront* he's antsy for leading-man roles even though we just cast him as Jud the heavy in *Oklahoma!* Our rivals over at MCA and William Morris call him ten times a day.

"Let Rod kick up his heels a bit—but keep him in the corral," Mary instructs me. "And speaking of corrals, we got him another western at Columbia, he's third banana after Glenn Ford. It isn't Chekhov but it pays."

Rod, in Mary's office now.

On cue I ease in, and nod, nod, nod, yes, yes, Rod is 100 percent correct as he complains about his stalled career. *The*

Big Knife, a recent Jaffe-inspired package where he played-
in-all-but-name my Columbia Pictures nemesis Harry Cohn,
with five of its main actors and the screenwriter all Jaffe
clients, well thank you very much, but today is now and
Steiger knows we like treadmilling him in routine pictures
to keep commissions flowing. "For this I studied under Lee
Strasberg and Gadge at the Actors Studio?"

Mary gives me her three-alarm-fire glance and I chime
in that we can't evade the issue, what about that important
Norman Mailer project, *The Naked and the Dead*, over at
Fox?

I'm making it up. The Mailer book is unfilmable.

Steiger is interested. He stops moaning. Unfortunately,
he's also literate. "Am I Sergeant Croft, Lieutenant Hearn,
or General Cummings?" he asks, naming the novel's three
main characters. Actors read?

This is why I'm the agency fireman, no compliment. I
improvise a line that Rod is too young for the fascist general and too handsome for the sadistic sergeant but he'd be
perfect for Hearn the idealistic lieutenant, which isn't true.

Mary's sigh of relief is almost audible.

She says, "Clancy, take Rod out to lunch."

Rod Steiger is a "downstairs problem" for actors' agents
like Ace Kantor. However, I'm often brought in to meet,
greet, pacify, and load up with literary material our roster
of disenchanted actors and directors who are easy prey for
other agencies. Under orders, and reading Mary's eye signs,
I take Rod out for a meal to bullshit him back to us.

❖

ON THE WAY down to the company parking lot and
Mary's borrowed Cadillac, I check out Steiger, a stubby,
barrel-chested, crinkle-haired bruiser who was a destroyer
deckhand in the Pacific War. He has a way of listening—
hooded eyes until they flip open in feigned wonder or real
surprise, with a veiled threat in there somewhere—or am I
influenced by his Charley Malloy, Brando's brother? And
since I rarely distinguish between reel and real life, Steiger is
an actor to fear.

I take him to Mocambo, the last surviving Sunset Strip
club, which the younger agents ignore as Old School but
still draws the senior guys. As I let the red-vested valet park
Mary's convertible, Rod grunts a laugh. "It wasn't so long
ago I ate out of garbage cans from places like this." Well, all
that's over, we'll see to that, my agent spiel. "No," he stops
me in the foyer and gives me the cold Charley Malloy stare.
"*I'll* see to that."

Lunch with clients is where I shine but Steiger won't let
up about the Mailer novel. And anyway I made it all up,
God knows who owns the rights. Let's change the subject to
him, usually clients love talking about themselves, but not
Steiger, he's serious.

"Come on," he urges me. "What am I, a schmuck? You
get me the Mailer and I'll do your *trafe*. But you get me
the Mailer. I will hold you personally responsible. Croft or
Hearn. I can play the sergeant so audiences will understand

him. I served in the Pacific under guys with that kind of mentality."

While eating I spot several guys from rival agencies salivating over Rod and I move protectively closer to him in our booth. "Trust me," I tell him, "it will happen. I'll make it happen."

Afterwards, back at the office, I tell Mary that Steiger wouldn't let go of the Mailer thing.

Uh oh. *The Naked and the Dead* died the death at all the studios. "Say *Kaddish* for it, Kid. What did you promise Rod?"

"I lied."

She grins. And shakes her head in mock chastisement. "He'll remember."

I get up to go.

"But I won't," I say.

❖

THE NAKED AND *the Dead* (1958) is finally made into a dreadful movie with shared blame by RKO and Warners. Aldo Ray plays the sergeant, Cliff Robertson the liberal lieutenant, and Raymond Massey—a Jaffe client—the heartless general.

26

Who Served, Who Didn't

BEHIND HER BACK we poke fun at Mary Baker's military tic calling us her platoon and all that, but there's a pride in her men who served in uniform. Nobody at the office, except shell-shocked Flip Edwards, ever speaks of his war experience, which anyway is fading. But it pleases me to work in the same business as, and try to find jobs for, former servicemen who include some pretty unlikely heroes. Even the singin' cowboy Gene Autry flew missions over the Burma Road, and pretty boy Tyrone Power was a Marine fighter pilot; Douglas Fairbanks Jr., he of the elegant tuxedo movies, was a British commando, as was our client David Niven. Henry Fonda at thirty-seven saw Pacific action, Clark Gable way over the age limit at forty-two went on many air combat missions, Sterling Hayden was a Marine dropped behind enemy lines, Robert Montgomery served on Pacific PT boats, Alec Guinness commanded a D-Day invasion boat, Glenn Ford fought with the French Resistance.

The writer Budd Schulberg helped liberate the death camps and captured the Nazi filmmaker Leni Riefenstahl.

Those were the officers. A special salute snaps off to the lowly enlisted men: Audie Murphy; Lew Ayres (pacifist but served as a medic in the Philippines); Kirk Douglas and Tony Curtis, US navy; Van Heflin, artillery; Walter Matthau and Sabu "the Indian Boy" flew missions; Ernest Borgnine, four years in navy combat; Charles Bronson, US Air Corps missions; Robert Ryan, a Marine drill sergeant; Charlton Heston, a bomber gunner; Lee Marvin, wounded Pacific marine; Jack Palance, injured air corps; Rod Steiger, on destroyers; and ugly-villain Neville Brand, the second-highest decorated soldier in the army after Audie Murphy. If you look at them on the screen you'll note the difference between someone who has seen war and someone who has not. To make an unfair point, compare the screen faces of Matt Damon, Ethan Hawke, Will Smith, etc., with, for example, Gene Hackman and Lee Marvin, who were Marines.

Three patriots—Ronald Reagan, John Wayne, and Ward Bond—stayed home.

27

Teacher's Pets

ON SATURDAY MORNINGS in the office, to bring a few of the unemployed up to speed, I run a private, invitation-only academy for four of my ruptured ducks who bring us little income but deserve our respect for services rendered. Subjects in my class include:

How to pitch a movie story in forty-five seconds by my new Swiss Roamer pearl-tone wristwatch and when to stop talking if the customer's eyelids flutter.

How to dress for success; no beatnik goatees, shoulder-length hair or berets, please.

How to research your prey. If your customer is a sports fisherman, mention you use a Royal Wulff or Parachute Adams fly. If a car buff, that you drive a first-production-model Harley Earl-designed Corvette.

How not to talk money unless I'm present.

"Clyde Simmons," ex-infantry private who looks remarkably like Eddie Slovik, the only GI ever executed for desertion, is a skin-and-bones Appalachian boy from the hills of Western Kentucky, five-foot-nothing and a survivor of rickets and TB, with a young wife and two daughters to support as well as an obsession to finish his "big American novel." They live in a converted chicken coop in Culver City. Having pawned his typewriter, he scribbles chapters of his novel in stub pencil on stolen Jaffe stationery. The coop stinks of chicken shit and so far I've failed to find him work. But an agent's mission is to make something out of nothing. On my list is another unemployed writer who was too old for the war, sixty-year-old "Len Leonard," with a string of forgotten credits but no income. Roll the dice, put Clyde and Len together in the same room and Hail Mary! They sell their very first script, then—as partners—a second and third. Clyde thanks me profusely because I have unlocked the money writer in him. "And what about your novel?" I ask. "What novel?" Clyde responds.

❖

BIG, RANGY JAMES Edmiston looks like, and is, a mountain man—and a human screenplay factory. A Pacific soldier who brought back a Japanese war bride and with his own hands built her a magnificent log cabin up by Yosemite—I've seen it—where they've raised a pack of children, he commutes in a war-surplus Jeep to a Sunset Strip motel he rents on a cheap monthly room rate in order to write undisturbed.

His Alta Loma Vue Motel a few doors down from the agency is basically a call-girl operation where the hookers drop in to offer Jim story ideas which he transcribes on a new-fangled IBM electric typewriter and a Thermofax copying machine, a crude affair that overheats, belching smoke and acrid-smelling fumes. On any given night or day, between sunset and dawn, Jim can originate a 120-page screenplay by banging it straight to the wax stencil. Next morning he'll show up on the Jaffe doorstep when our office opens with copies brass stapled and the ink still wet on pages. His work is derivative of a thousand pictures you've seen (true of 90 percent of what I sell), but anyway I like his looks: Buffalo Bill Cody chamois hunting jacket and eyes sparkling with the joy of the chase. Inevitably, late at night, in his motel room, the whores wandering in and out, we collaborate on a script, *The Golden Vanity*. (Think *Stagecoach* on uppers.) If you look very closely at westerns of the period, you may, if lucky, see whole swatches from *The Golden Vanity* here, there, and almost everywhere else.

Jim Edmiston I'd trust with my life, but "Danny Danowitz," ex-supply corporal, I wouldn't trust for ten seconds to be in a room alone with my wallet because he's a charmingly self-confessed plagiarizer and scam artist. I inherited him, spit curl and beach tan and all, from the agent whose office I now occupy. Danny has persuaded me, too, to partner with him on a script in my spare time, and since he's candid about stealing his previous partners' work and selling it as his own, I register-mail to myself each day's pages that we write together. The partnership implodes when he wonders why two guys in fedoras are hanging around the driveway of my new apartment. I say FBI. Danny races to the bathroom but not before demanding, "If you sell it, don't contact me. I'll let you know where to send my half of the money," and climbs out the rear window, shinnies down the drainpipe, and disappears through the shrubbery and down the alley, nevermore to be seen.

Finally, "Will Lawrence" is a war casualty twice over. All through the North Africa, Sicily, Italy, and D-Day campaigns he was a young officer in Graves Registration Command, in charge of collecting dog tags and burying what was left of corpses on Salerno, Anzio, Omaha Beach, and the Siegfried Line. Settled in postwar LA, married to Marie, a pisscutter of a wife whose mouth would make a Marine blush ("How are you tonight, y'old cocksucking fuckhead?"), he's famished for movie work. His problem is a phobic resistance to writing anything with dead bodies, which cancels him out for practically everything. Impatiently I ask, "What *will* you write?" Marie, who always accompanies him to my office, grins wickedly, "Go 'head, hon, tell the man, he's only tryin' to hep." (Marie, like her husband, is from Texas.) Will replies, "Wild blue yonder." Ah of course, up there in the sky it's clean and distant from the blood-drenched earth he spent four years digging up. When I try but fail to get him a proper job the three of us just go out and get horribly drunk a lot, and later, when things get really rough for them, he gives up screenwriting to write a book about stratospheric balloon flights at 96,000 feet above where the bodies are buried.

PART FOUR

28

Time Out of Time

I T'S ONE OF those strange Los Angeles late summer days when the city has relaxed into an unusual stretch of cool weather. Then without warning the sun strikes, hostile, unwavering, burning the skin as through a gigantic magnifying glass. It feels personal, as if the sun's death-ray has singled you out among the millions. Of course it's meteorological, an accident of high pressure and stagnant air trapping smoke from local raging brush fires high above the Malibu ridges and the more distant Angeles National Forest. Nobody is on the streets except old ladies wearing wet handkerchiefs as headgear and little children chasing an ice cream truck. All sane people are indoors or dead of asphyxiation.

Making my studio rounds in San Fernando's Death Valley on a day like this is like stepping into a furnace. How did the early movie makers like D.W. Griffith and Cecil B. DeMille, battling snakes, scorpions, dust, and flash floods, manage to make this parched ranchland a gigantic open-air movie studio? And charge admission! Sun, which is killing me, was their Muse.

29

Harmless as Doves; Innocent as a Lamb

Bud Abbott (as Peter Patterson): How stupid can you get?

Lou Costello (as Freddie Franklin): How stupid do you want me to be?

—From *Abbott & Costello Meet the Mummy* (1955)

T HE TALL THIN balding guy who is epileptic and the tubby little guy with the rheumatic heart are being strangled "Arrgghh!" in the blood-drenched claws of an ancient cloth-wrapped Egyptian mummy. Bud and Lou—the money-making machine known as "Abbott and Costello"— are in deep shit because they stole the sacred medallion from the tomb of Princess Ara, thus earning the wrath of evil Professor Zoomer and his curvy accomplice, Madame Rontru, and her monster mummy, Klaris. I loved these guys when I was a kid.

When my different lives fracture into so many pieces, I can't immediately recall who I am, and the FBI-inspired fear-rash on my back erupts like Krakatoa, and Terry accelerates her demands that we hit, spit, and curse each other, drawing blood—which is her way of annulling the political fear, and I'm losing her probably to men who can better satisfy her, I decompress, ease back, and go in for a form of anti-stress meditation on the back lots of my valley studios, to hang around the B-or-less budget sets, pit stops so relaxed nobody ever calls for security because the players are not glamorous stars requiring special protection.

The burnt-toast smell of plywood flats, cobra-thick electric cables, and the odd perfume of whirring 35mm Mitchell cameras is pure Chanel No. 5.

After a day of being thrown out of producers' offices ("No, NO! FUCKINGNOWAY!! Cocksuckin' agents!!") I lounge in the Assistant Director's canvas chair on Stage 16 to observe that bloodcurdling Mormon hussy, Marie Windsor, shove helpless Lou Costello onto a rug-covered couch and slobber him with distracting kisses while she searches his Humpty Dumpty frame for the Medallion of Evil.

"Oh-h-h-h, Abbott!!" Lou yodels his trademark girlish scream to his partner of twenty years and around forty films together. This will be the duo's next to last picture for Universal. They've run their course, are overexposed, have moved on to TV, and both of them look ill. Lou, the fat one with his bad heart, looks so tired it's hard to picture him as what he used to be, a first-rate boxer and stunt man. Both Lou and Bud are totally exhausted.

Why do they do it? They're rich and famous and their act has long gone stale. Ace Kantor, Jaffe's #1 actor's agent, tells me (a) work is their habit, (b) they're in hock to the IRS even though each has been among the highest paid in Hollywood. Maybe it's why Lou goes around on each of his sets demanding that everyone sign an anti-Communist petition. You get fired if you don't sign.

I also hang around the Ma and Pa Kettle series where Ma is played by the veteran character actress Marjorie Main, who'll stroll out of shot from the fake-front farmhouse and plump herself on a canvas chair next to mine and ask, "Wanna play gin rummy? I wasn't raised to cheat, but I sure do."

Main, who has built an Academy Award career out of playing bawling battleaxes, can after a day's work transform herself into a stunning older woman in stylish street clothes, always with white gloves, like my mom. She may be only a character actress but out in the rural one-theater towns, she's a mega-star. She really does remind me of Jennie, who drags home after a day at Catalina Swimwear looking worn and haggard, but a bath and an hour later before launching herself on a date, can look quite glam.

❖

BETWEEN TAKES, MAIN is terrific company as we deal gin rummy and, yes, she does cheat. While shuffling cards (some from the bottom of the deck), she converses to someone over my shoulder who is, she confides, her dead husband, and she has been known to do so in the middle of takes. "My pictures make so much money in Grand Rapids they're afraid to tell me I'm a crazy old bitch," she crows.

Aside from talking to the dead, and probably being lesbian (her main squeeze, sitting alongside me, is the fluttery actress Spring Byington), Marjorie seems extraordinarily comfortable with herself, which neither Abbott nor Costello are, given their IRS and health problems. She's been working steadily for forty years of paychecks, a miracle in our business.

It's enchanting to be around all these vaudeville stage veterans who've knocked about in every fourth-rate burlesque house from Altoona to Zuni and refuse to worry themselves into an early grave with the stress of being a celebrity. Their ratty movie sets are so tension-free that I never want to go back to my Ultra-Moderne office with its client anxieties and bee-buzzing phones. Here I can wander in, take a pew out of camera range, and simply wait for someone to chat me up.

I'm also free to wander my other patrol sectors—Republic, and lowly Producers Releasing Corporation (PRC, Pretty Rotten Crap), Monogram, Liberty Bell, Mascot, or Allied Artists—the dinky little independent, less-than-no-budget studios to whom I sell my clients' pulp magazine stories for fifty bucks apiece. I'm in love, no other word for it, with my earliest horseback heroes, aging cowboy stars like Colonel Tim McCoy whose quick draw takes only six frames out of the 24-frames-per-second; Bob Steele; and ten-times-married former hairdresser Lash La Rue who like me lied his way into movies, in his case by pretending to be a bullwhip virtuoso. And if there's one amazing director I can watch, I mean study, to see how it's really done, it's Sam Newfield, an obscure Poverty Gulch dynamo who grinds 'em out so fast the studio has to release his pictures under aliases. What is he on that without breathing hard he puts in the can twenty films a year, like *Blazing Frontier* and *Mask of the Dragon*?

Newfield's is the sub-sub-culture that never gets mentioned at the agency because there's little money and zero prestige in it for us; Jaffe takes pride in its distinguished list of Academy Award winners and Sam Newfield might tarnish the stardust. But who can deny Newfield's magic touch that gives work to horror stars of yesterday like super-villain George Zucco (What? You don't know him as Professor Moriarty in the Sherlock Holmes series?) and vamps like Evelyn Ankers, Mary Beth Hughes, Maria Montez (queen of the cobras), iconic and irreplaceable? That's picture making.

What will really make my day is running into the gold standard of monsters, Boris Karloff, the original Frankenstein miscreation, so when it's rumored that he's at Universal shooting *Abbott and Costello Meet Dr. Jekyll and Mr. Hyde* I drive like crazy onto the still-under-construction Hollywood Freeway to the Valley.

IT'S AMAZING THE blacklisters haven't come after Karloff, an outspoken union man who, when asked, is all for the British "socialized" health system. Just imagine: the monster shaking the bars in the same prison with the Hollywood Ten. The conversations they'd have!

On Stage 8, A&C are playing two dumb American cops in Victorian London pursuing Karloff's evil Mr. Hyde.

(The lead screenwriter soon will be blacklisted.) Offstage Costello reads the *New York Times* stock market quotations, Bud drowses, and Karloff, a gentleman in Victorian-era costume, waits for his cue. I stroll across the set to quietly sit next to The Monster as he scrutinizes the action with a scholarly eye.

Lou chases Bud, Bud chases Lou. In that world-famous lisp Karloff the actor sighs to nobody in particular, "Poor Robert Louis Stevenson."

Is Fu Manchu, the Mummy, and Frankenstein's creature, speaking to me?

And can I steal him from his current agent and bring the monster's dripping head to lay at the feet of Mary Baker . . . ?

How to break the ice is always the problem. The standard lie rolls easily off an agent's tongue: "I'm with the Jaffe Office, Mister Karloff. We talk about you all the time at meetings. If you ever are unhappy . . ." Wrong move.

The Monster honors me, yes that's how it feels, with a look, to be truthful an icy glare—the same kind Woody Strode daggered me with in *Bride of the Gorilla* when I showed up in blackface. Mr. Karloff rises in faint disgust and tromps off to his dressing room to change from Dr. Jekyll into Mr. Hyde, fangs, hairy skin, and all. Universal is so cheap they use parts of a leftover costume from *The Wolfman*. Stupid me. Missed my chance. Poor William Henry Pratt (Karloff's real name), ace gardener, the scariest Im-ho-tep of them all, teacher of my youth, militant actors' guild member, isn't acting when he lurches and limps away with his bad back, injured when the studio forced his feet in iron shoes and a ton of makeup for the James Whale classic.

Farewell, faithful fiend.

❖

ON THE ADJOINING Stage 9 our client Donald O'Connor is second banana to a real live mule in *Francis in the Navy*, one of a Francis-the-talking-mule series that's a money spinner in the sticks except that lately Donald has somersaulted into the Jaffe office complaining that the animal gets more fan mail than him. This will be his last mule picture, which is a pity, since we get steady commissions from this absurdity.

Everyone at Jaffe adores O'Connor, who leaps and pratfalls over our waiting-room barrier and wonders why, after his success in *Singin' in the Rain* and that spectacular "Make 'em Laugh" number we can't find him a classier job than co-starring with a talking animal. Who can blame him?

Donald, in a boyish sailor uniform, is in the midst of a take with his arm around the sleepy (tranquillized?) mule when I amble onto the set. Just off camera, the mule's caretaker is manipulating a nearly invisible thread tied to the mule's lips or teeth to make the animal's mouth quiver, which later will be synced by the actor Chill Wills' dubbed voice in a sound booth.

In between takes, to entertain the crew and pinch himself awake, a visibly bored Donald leans on the animal, holds his nose against an imaginary mule fart, crosses his eyes, dislocates his jaw: the classic O'Connor inventory. Then he dumps himself into the chair a couple over from mine.

"Um, Mister O'Con . . . Donald . . ."

He squirms in the canvas chair in a way that tangles his head and feet so that somehow he's upside down.

I try again. "Um, I'm with the Jaffe—"

". . . and no anchovies but lots of cheese."

He untangles himself so that he twists himself into an even more improbable human knot, literally peeking up his own asshole.

"Womb with a view!" he cackles in his mule voice.

Is he always "on" and where does he get his pep? Like Buster Keaton, he's already an old man in showbiz terms, having done it from the cradle.

I schmooze how much we at Jaffe admire him.

"Well, mighty nice of you. I'm Sam Jaffe, who are you? Oh, Donald O'Connor. Fabulous dramatic actor." He stares gloomily at his upraised hand. "Is this a dagger I see before me? It is the East, and Juliet is the sun! Arise, fair sun, and kill the envious moon. O, that this too, too solid flesh would melt, thaw, and resolve itself into a dew. I dew, do yew?"

And then he's called back into a scene with the mule. He nuzzles up to it and coos just before the camera starts rolling, "Ah, wuvs oo, darlin'."

Ah wuvs oo, too, Donald.

30

The Big Steal

"FELLAS, LET'S FACE it, they're killing us in today's
market." Sam Jaffe, founder and head of the agency,
ruddy and balding, is a picture of measured health as he
faces us all leaning his sturdy back against a desk in his spa-
cious ground-floor office at the foot of the circular iron
steps. He is flanked by his two partners: Mary Baker, and his
brother-in-law Phil Gersh.

Tuesday mornings are religious inspirationals disguised
as obligatory staff conferences. It's where the real business
gets done. And where I learn the rules and how to break
them.

My thirteen brother agents slouch in chairs in a semi-
circle around Mr. Jaffe, munching Danish and slurping
from Styrofoam coffee cups, restless to leave the office and
earn their bonuses while secretaries including Addy and my
receptionist Joanna stand with poised notebooks, and at Mr.
Jaffe's elbow the office manager, "Princess," is maliciously

alert to note down our mishaps and mistakes especially anyone's failure to return calls the same day, Jaffe's sin of sins.

Staff meetings are a primitive tribal ritual. An agent who announces a new (or former) client stolen (or re-stolen) from a rival agency, thus displaying the enemy's head on the village pole, is seen as embodying a special life force and earns an extra tranche of bonus.

My X-ray eyes distractedly scan anyone who might call my bluff, puncture my balloon, and reveal me as a fraud. I brood endlessly about where I fit into the team; I'm still looking for an edge, a trademark style, a way of performing. I audition myself all the time in front of a mirror with gestures, intonations, timing. So far my only corporate asset is what Mary Baker calls steel balls: I'll go anywhere, do or say anything to close a deal. I'm in charge of "cold cases," scripts hitherto impossible to sell, but I hit lucky my second week by randomly plucking from the pile—and selling— *Cattle Queen of Montana*, which made me that week's boy. Chemical euphoria—speed pills for breakfast, Dexxies and Benzies for lunch washed down by White Horse in buttermilk—accounts for the "enthusiasm" Sam admires so much. He still can't get over my slugging the William Morris agent as an example of loyalty to the firm.

"Need I tell you? We're vulnerable to raids," Mr. Jaffe repeats.

A muted groan around the room.

Mr. Jaffe hammers us: "Face it, fellas, an outstanding client list we got, okay? Academy Awards up to here. But—need

I tell you?—not young any more. Bogie, Freddie March, Joe Cotten, Joan Fontaine. They work steady, keep us in commissions and you guys in brisket. Need I tell you? We lost half our income when the *harah* (shit) came to town"—Sam yanks a bathtowel-sized handkerchief from his breast pocket and goes "Pfui!" in a shtetl gesture of pretending to spit and tosses it contemptuously in a waste basket—"and damn near wiped us out. Crucified our best people. Communists! Feh! Most talented, best quotes, sweetest deals." He never refers to HUAC except as an expletive.

"Speaking of which, Mary and I want all you guys in on this, the temperature of the times is, *Grapes of Wrath* and *Best Years of Our Lives*, sure, all those Academies and good box-office too, is not where our market is today. Even Sabu the Indian Boy is making anti-communist movies. Yesterday's stool pigeons today's heroes. You know, 'I Was a Schmegege for the FBI', okay okay I know the title, and *My Son John*? Box office dogs but you gotta show the flag. Mary, encourage your writers, okay?"

Mary says, "Sam, we don't tell our writers what to write. They're creative people."

Sam sighs for effect. "So let them be creative a little more . . ." he searches for a word . . . "American. You know that picture *High Noon*. Don't remind me, Gary Cooper in the movie is a hero but in front of the *harah* did the dirty. His deputy Lloyd Bridges, same. If it happened in real life, you know, the villain Frank Miller, would shoot the marshall, rape the widow and people in the town would run to kiss Miller's ass. That's *real* life in Hollywood!"

HE WANDERS AMONG us flinging his arms like his client
Raymond Massey playing an Old Testament prophet and
punching the air for emphasis.

"So! We never rest! We go to parties! And to premieres.
Telephone callbacks, when? SAME DAY that's when! Give
service. We keep what we have and bring in younger clients.
That's your department, Clancy."

Tired nods all around.

"WAKE UP, FELLAS! Let me hear it! What's our edge
over MCA and William Morris?" He cups his hand to his ear.

Someone mumbles, "Um . . ."

"Goddam right! Re-ci-pro-city . . . teamwork . . . esprit
de corps . . . BAND OF BROTHERS!" Mr. Jaffe gazes down
at us fondly. Draws a breath. "Side by side, back to back,
Spartans at Thermopylae." He turns to Zack Silver the ex-
classics man. "Or was it at Marathon, Zachariah?"

Zack retorts, "It's Greek to me, Sam. Either way we head
them off at Apache Pass," a reference to our staple income
selling "horse operas" especially if there's a role for any of
our B-actor clients, like Steve Cochran, Wendell Corey, Ray
Danton, Vince Edwards, Vic Morrow, Dale Robertson, any
male who can sit in a saddle without falling off, and in a
pinch we'll throw in one or two Indian chiefs, usually actors
of Jewish or Italian origin with big pecs. Few westerns are
written by real Westerners; some of the quickest sales are
done by geeky Jewish boys from Brooklyn.

❖

Now, the point of it all.

"WHO'S OUT OF WORK?" Clients and what we haven't done for them.

We cough, sip coffee, recross legs, prepare excuses, study the carpet.

So many elephants in the room: movie-ticket admissions falling, foreign markets in the toilet . . . and as for television Sam sticks a finger down his throat to gag:

"Smell-o-vision!"

Sam and I both are TV snobs, contemptuous of its moron's menu of kiddie shows and perfumed wrestlers, except the economic reality is that TV production is moving west to LA from New York, a squawking chicken waiting to be plucked by MCA's crafty Lew Wasserman but not by us. Our own TV-centric agents—"Ted Morgan" (field artillery, East Coast money) and "Lloyd Harrigan" (army Chemical Corps, USC varsity lineman)—must be the most frustrated men in Hollywood.

Sam Jaffe—who came up in the silent Buster Keaton–Garbo era—and I are passionately committed to an increasingly obsolete business model of star-driven, machine-made dramas and comedies crafted by tyrant-run studio factories on an assembly line and shown in theaters "tied" to the movie-making company.

Sam orates: ". . . *We few, we happy few, we band of brothers . . .*" and he goes right on through Shakespeare's Henry V speech . . . "*And gentlemen in England now abed/ Shall think themselves accused they were not here . . .*"

Sam turns to Mary Baker. "Did I get it right?" Mrs. Baker, in a light gray Dior suit and Hattie Carnegie banded straw floppy fedora over one eye, her full lips a snarling slash of bright red lipstick, nods.

"Yes, Sam," in a cigarette voice, "except it's 'accursed' not 'accused.'"

Jaffe is pleased to be corrected in public by the head of his literary department. Although he's now a wealthy, superbly barbered Renoir-collecting member of Hollywood royalty, he's basically still a tough little tenement-bred Jew from Delancy Street and the only one of the town's elite agents— Wasserman, Abe Lastfogel, Swifty Lazar, etc.—with hands-on experience actually making movies. As Paramount's former production manager responsible for fifty pictures a year, he invented night-for-day shooting, saving the studio from bankruptcy, while dating Greta Garbo and the silent super-sex-star Clara Bow. What a player.

Trouble is, he has unrealistic expectations of his youngest and newest hire, me.

Winding up he shoots me a reproachful glance, "You, Clancy, where do you spend your nights? I never see you at openings or parties. You know how many deals are made standing at the pisser in the men's room of the Pantages? That old gent with a bad prostate next to you is dying to give you his money, only you have to get in there with him. Flatter him! Make him feel warm and loved! You have a god-given gift for literary bullshit and they love it when you talk Spinoza or Shakespeare or . . ."

"Herman Wouk?" suggests Jonathan Buck with a straight face.

"Do we represent Wouk?" Sam asks in surprise.

"No."

"Fuck him, let's move on," Sam says.

"Speaking of clothes," Sam changes gears, "Zanuck just bought *The Man in the Gray Flannel Suit* for Greg Peck. See if there's a role for Freddy March and Lee Cobb . . ."

Ace Kantor clears his throat. "Um, Sam, a Lee Cobb problem. Skouras at Fox. Hates commies. And they just had this *tsores* with Elia Kazan . . ."

Mr. Jaffe explodes: "Skouras should talk! How long did that *nar* go to prison for extortion? *Ayin kafin yan!*" (He should go shit in the ocean: Mary is teaching me, fast.) Skouras the Fox chief was jailed for paying off union gangsters in an extortion plot.

Elia Kazan . . . Reds . . . commies . . . betrayals . . . the never-spoken-aloud problem of blacklist . . . an unheard sigh around the crowded room. I gulp my cold Styrofoam coffee pretending as if a ghost has not breathed on my neck.

Zack Silver: "Isn't Lee cleared?"

Cleared.

Jonny says, "Yeah. Martin Gang."

Mrs. Baker: "Ah, the magic words."

Martin Gang, the inquisitor's best friend, *consigliere* to the mega-stars and rainmaker to the respectable Jewish community, a Beverly Hills lawyer, what else?, for a fee he'll arrange with the Dark God himself—FBI chief J. Edgar

Hoover—for a client to "clear" himself by confessing and repenting to any sin on the menu.

Poor Lee Cobb with his bad heart, forced or forcing himself to do the dirty on his best friends.

Words fly around the room, taken down by Princess and the secretaries to be enscrolled on green tissue inter-office memos: deals, open jobs, unavailabilities, quotes, *force majeure*, gripes, excuses, boasts, promises, sighs. The Lorre problem . . . the Palance problem . . . the Ida Lupino and Dorothy McGuire and Rhonda Fleming problems . . .

Barbara Stanwyck's name comes up. Someone mutters, "She's all washed up."

Sam cries aloud in real anguish, "Nobody is ever washed up. Don't you ever let me hear you say washed up or over the hill. You do not have the right to condemn a person for a lifetime. We don't know."

❖

STANWYCK'S NAME HITS a nerve. Sam knows how we think. Who's hot and who's cold? It is engraved in letters of fire on our brains. With his long experience of hot turning cold and vice versa, careers in the dumps that suddenly rise phoenix-like, his task is to drill past our cemented-in mindset, a job killer if we let it.

Sam brings it home. "You are responsible for the livelihoods of people—never give up on a client!" He turns to his brother-in-law and partner Phil Gersh. "You were at Anzio when Kesselring tried to push you guys off the beach. But never surrendered, right?"

Phil says, "The Germans were a pushover compared to Selznick."

That wraps it up. We stir to take up our duties. But first, the Talmudic Ritual.

Sam paces among us.

"Finally, fellas, need I tell you? In America the pie is big enough for everybody! Sufficient unto." He spreads out his arms to indicate size. "Beat the other guy's brains out, kick him in the balls, drag him into a ditch . . . but never over into bankruptcy. Never!"

❖

KASHRUT. SAM, LIKE many of his first generation, was raised in a traditional Jewish home where *kashrut*, the ancient Hebraic kosher-food commandment, is also translated as dealing fairly, if sometimes brutally, in business, justice honored in word if not always in deed. This eternal, unresolvable conflict between kosher—what's decent—and *trafe*—unclean—is in his bones.

Sam clasps his hands. Here it comes. He loves this part.

"You know, fellas, from before your time, I did locations in Griffith Park for *I Am a Fugitive From a Chain Gang*."

Sam lowers his voice dramatically.

"It's night in the city. Police sirens in the distance. Bloodhounds. This Academy Award–winning actor Paul

Muni—an escaped convict—our former client, take my
word one day he'll walk back in—is hunted and hungry.
Out of the dark mist he emerges . . ." Sam pauses for effect.
". . . to say farewell to the girl he loves." He pauses again.

Sam: "She begs him, 'But how will you live . . .'?"

Sam: "And he says what?"

ALL OF US, from the heart: "I STEAL!"

All that talk about clearances, blacklist, purges . . . A
spectral breath tickles the back of my neck . . . At such
moments I struggle to keep a straight face because I'm such
a repeat offender.

31

The Demon Barber of Wilshire Boulevard

T HESE DAYS, AS commanded by Sam and Mary, who insist we get our hair done military style, close and tight, I get a weekly trim, a new experience for me and my paisan barber, "Tommy May."

Tommy cranks me down in his hydraulic leather-and-metal barber chair and then gives such a twirl I have to grip its arms. "*Mincha!*" he curses in Sicilian. "What gives you the right to work when the rest of us aren't?"

His real name is Tomasso Magliocco (Screen Actors Guild name: Tommy May), a hunky, feral-faced Sicilian-American, the haircutter of choice for LA's blacklisted colony. His tidy one-man shop, in the basement of a Wilshire Boulevard medical building that also houses a score of black-listed doctors and dentists—dismissed by their hospitals and partnerships—is where we outcasts kick back, loosen up, throw off the masks of whatever disguises we're currently wearing, and breathe easier under Tommy's expertly applied hot towel. He is a master of the ancient village art of "cupping," placing white-hot glass tumblers on the naked skin of your back and neck to draw out the evil toxins. Tommy can drive out everyone's demons but his own.

Tommy May whips off my Van Heusen coral linen shirt to examine the raw red rash down my naked spine which I pretend is from a sexually transmitted disease and not what it really is, fear pimples triggered by the FBI's nocturnal visits. Sometimes I puke and shit afterwards, too. Some hero.

Tommy is an authentic hoodlum, a side-of-the-mouth shoulder-holster killer on the Twentieth Century Limited racing through the moonless night or in a sordid gangland alley—any movie location where he's called on to hit his chalk mark and snarl, "Okay, copper—keep your hands where I can see 'em. You're on a fast track to hell."

After soul-killing years of auditions and no callbacks, this street kid from New York's Hell's Kitchen finally established himself as a dramatic presence in a string of movie thrillers . . . when boom! He's torpedoed by a House Un-American Activities Committee subpoena to which his response is a defiant obscene speech carried front page by the *LA Times* and *Herald-Express* whereupon his agent, Sam Jaffe, sacks him, the home phone goes dead, and with a family to support he returns to his father's trade, *i capelli e rasoio*, the comb and razor.

He's got the Mary Baker habit: at 10 A.M. he's already bombed.

Tommy's basement is a salon of sorts for outlaw men and women so you never know who you'll meet here, a Communist fugitive or a fired sportswriter or a disgraced studio electrician or some poor bastard who signed a petition and is still wondering what hit him. I belong here, but yet don't, the **nine names** still tucked inside my wallet, yet here I am, among the people I may betray.

As I recline in his swivel chair, Tommy goes into his act, which he likes doing when pissed, angry, or bored. Acting was his passion, the culmination of boyhood dreams, a soul validation, and now he has no audience except his customers. His forefinger presses gun-hard against my temple as he growls, in his movie-gangster bass: ". . . if I find out you did the squeal job on me I'll blow your brains out and feed them to the fishes, got me?" That coldblooded menacing snarl took him from Eleventh Avenue to RKO.

He's pretending. I hope.

Curious, I ask if the "other ones," the informers, ever come in? Every family has one.

"Yeah, you'd be surprised," Tommy responds in his normal voice. "Some make a trip special, one guy all the way from San Diego. Revisit the crime scene. Always leave a big tip. One *ragazzaccio* left a ten spot. I threw it on the floor. But picked it up after he was gone. The motherfuckin' *rompicoglioni*."

"Where's your pride?" I needle him.

"Where's your tip, *gabola*?"

A week later, I'm back down in Tommy's shop to find him holding an old-fashioned straight razor to the throat of a customer whose face is hidden under a hot towel.

In his on-camera mode, he gives the customer in the swivel chair a slow whirl following it in a crazy dance step with an upraised razor.

"How do you want it—rat?" He loves quoting from old scripts.

Under the towel, the guy, I can only see his trouser cuffs, chuckles along with the gag. Tommy glances at me to make a throat-cutting gesture. He leans in to the customer. "Either way you croak—slow or fast?"

"Tommy," the toweled guy's muffled voice, "you're brilliant."

Tommy's bloodshot eyes stare down at the customer.

"Clancy," Tommy announces, "meet this prince of a fellow. Martin Berkeley."

Whoa, impressive! Martin Berkeley should be in the Guinness Book of Records. He vomited up the names of no fewer than 155 friends, family, and strangers, some of whom he'd never met, most of whom had their careers and, in some cases their lives, wrecked. A hypersnitch rewarded with screenwriting jobs (*Tarantula, Revenge of the Creature*) for another "friendly" HUAC witness, the producer William Alland at one of my studios, Universal.

WATCHING MARTIN BERKELEY under Tommy's hot towel, my agent's mind quickly calculates his "quote," probably a low $650 a week. Is he happy with his agent or "vulnerable" . . . ? Stop it, Clancy. Have some morals.

"Tommy's a great kidder," says Berkeley, sitting upright as the barber removes the towel to brush-lather his face with shaving cream, making him look like Father Christmas.

Tommy leans in very close to him. "Who's kidding, Marty?" Unsteady on his feet, he makes a circular motion with the razor near Berkeley's ear.

"When's my turn, Tommy?" I call out as a cease-and-desist.

"Let me finish off this guy first," he says.

Tommy has maybe thirty pounds on me so if I grab the razor, Berkeley could end up a gory mess on the checkerboard lino floor.

Under the lather Berkeley probably has stopped smiling. He leans rigidly against the back of the chair and stares at the floating razor through white foam eyeslits.

"Tommy!" I shout. "Cut—"

Wrong word.

"—I mean, it's a wrap. Douse the lights. Print it."

Tommy comes to. His bleary eyes focus, and he straightens up to begin shaving his customer, *very* carefully. When finished he whips the sheet off Berkeley with a ritual flourish. Berkeley gets up and shakily goes to the clothes hook on the wall, grabs his sports jacket and heads for the elevators.

Tommy coughs. "That's two dollars, sir."

At the glass door Berkeley reaches into his back pocket for his wallet, pulls out two bills, hands them over, and backs out of the shop. "Thanks, Tommy. See you around."

Tommy, his evil movie grin: "Not if I see you first."

After Berkeley is gone, Tommy flourishes the bills in his hand: two tens—that's twenty dollars for a two-buck haircut.

"Not bad," I say. "He bought you."

Tommy stands by the empty barber chair sharpening the straight razor on the leather strop hanging from it. Back and forth, back and forth. He tests the razor on his thumb.

And looks at me completely sober. The look of a priest, not a friend.

"And who's buying you?"

❖

IN THIS VAST cosmology of informers there are exquisite ranks, grades, reasons, excuses. Do they voluntarily engage in the destruction of their friends or are they dragged unwilling? Informing in public or private sessions? Maximum or minimum damage? What degree of pressure is applied? A family to shield . . . a sick child . . . an institutionalized wife? Blackmailed? Do they take pleasure or pain from betraying? The eternal problem of guilt, assigned or evaded.

32

A Double Life

I NEVITABLY, MY SEPARATE worlds collide.

❖

THE PHONE SHRILLY rings intruding on a Friday night
Omega meeting at my new second-floor balcony upstairs
apartment at the Andalusia Gardens, a near replica of Bogart's
hideaway in *In a Lonely Place* (1950), which Ray and I have
seen half a dozen times because we are the deranged hero
Dixon Steele barely in control of our violences.

Sam Jaffe's voice crackles on the tapped line. "Clancy,
get your *toochis* down to the Beverly Wilshire hotel. Sheree
North's date didn't show up. And Louella and Bogie are getting sloshed. You may have to take her home."

Who, Sheree? "No, Louella." And hangs up.

Bogie is our best-earning client, Sheree North our bid
against Marilyn Monroe's increasingly fragile stardom, we
hope.

My Omega gang is amused to see how in a controlled
panic I respond to Sam Jaffe's whistle, scramble into the
clothes closet where I hide Zack's angry wife's .38 under
a pile of sweaters; drag out the tux Mary made me buy;
struggle into it and a new pair of Florsheims; duck into the
bathroom to swallow my nightly ration of Benzies, Tuinal,
Miltown and take a swallow of the White Horse I keep in
a Listerine bottle; and dash out the front door taking the
front tile steps three at a time, twisting a red cummerbund
around my waist while trying to snap on my snap-on bow
tie at the same time. I toss a jaunty salute to any Federal
car that may or may not be lurking under the ficus trees,
dive into the basement garage, roll into my Pontiac, and
ten minutes later I'm in the grand ballroom of the Beverly
Wilshire hotel for the after-premiere party of Bogart's *The
Barefoot Contessa*.

"What kept you?" Sam whispers, steering me into a
small group that includes Bogart, his wife Lauren Bacall,
my date Sheree North, and Mary Baker stunning in a form-
fitting royal-blue knit cocktail dress, high neck, long sleeves,
wide skirt: a knockout.

But the queen of our little entourage is a chipmunk-
cheeked, stout middle-aged woman imperially resplendent
in a floor-length Ben Reig silver satin, rhinestone-beaded
cocktail dress and a jeweled tiara in her hair and a brooch
the size of a Napoleonic medal on her matronly chest.

Even before I can slip my arm around lovely Sheree, the
woman grabs me and holds on.

"Schmuck," Sam mutters under his breath. "Smile. Louella's your new date. Drunk as a skunk. Take care of her."

"What about Sheree?" I whisper.

"What Lolly wants she gets," Sam says.

The lady grips me for dear life. How could I have failed to recognize the nationally syndicated Hearst newspaper gossip columnist who is more famous than the celebrities she chatters about in her also syndicated radio show ("Hel-LO, America! You heard it here first! Darling Judy Garland tells me rumors of trouble on *A Star Is Born* are just unfounded speculation . . . ! . . . Poor Susan Hayward's marriage to Jess Barker is heading for the rocks . . . !!")

Louella Parsons, queen/matriarch of vipers, arbiter of morals, with a single typewriter keystroke can make or break careers, poking under a star's bed to find incriminating crumbs, but servile to studio publicity machines in censoring items potentially damaging to celebrity investments, racing against her one-time protégé, equally dragon-tongued columnist Hedda Hopper, to see who can save America first. Famously, Lolly despises commies, liberals, intellectuals, and Catholics of her faith who break the church's sexual rules. The blacklist fear that rules Hollywood gives her extraordinary power.

I've hit the jackpot. Is Sam crazy to put us two together?

We're just standing around, Bogie and Lauren and Lolly and Sam and Mary and Sheree and me, lifting drinks from trays lofted by traveling waiters in a ballroom crowded with well-wishers, studio execs, hangers-on, and a few selected photographers.

I love being here. They accept me.

The Devil loosens my tongue. "Love your column, Lolly." I give her a manly hug and stare down her capacious bosom behind the chocolate-lace bodice. She has a way of grimacing a public-adores-me grin that reminds me of Bette Davis just before she fires point blank into an unfaithful lover.

"Dance?" I ask. There's a small combo at the other end of the ballroom playing wallpaper jazz.

Sam shoots me a don't-you-dare look.

In a glassy-eyed way Louella is interested in me as we sway together, arm in arm, in sync, her perplexed stare fixed on my flushed-with-three-scotches face, as if registering it for deadline copy. I'm so happy, with my arm around the stars' loving tormentor, movieland's #1 inquisitor. I'm in. Not sober, but *in*.

Then, ever so gradually, in my ears, a faint "zipping" sound like a bedsheet tearing softly. Z-z-z-z-p.

I chat away, Louella sways, smiles, frowns, smiles, frowns, hard to tell the difference. For all she cares I could be reciting from *Das Kapital*.

The "z-z-z-p" sound persists and grows louder. Nobody else in our little party, including Bogart and Bacall, pays it any mind, so it must not be happening.

Then, my nose flares to a slightly acrid odor. A definite aroma. I look around . . . and down. A puddle is forming at Louella Parsons's expensive, baby-blue cocktail shoes. It grows larger and becomes a trickle that inches slowly away from under her to Bogart who, without pausing in mid-sentence, nimbly shifts his hip into Bacall's to let the liquid move past him.

The odor is quite strong now.

Louella is pissing, hugely, drunkenly, in her pants.

The cocktail chatter goes on. Only Sheree's eyes widen. I turn away and warn, "Sam."

He whispers in my ear, "You see *goornisht*. Nothing."

"But Mr. Jaffe—"

Bogart turns to me and in that world-famous prison-lisp, ever so quietly: "Relax, Kid. She does it all the time. Pisses on us."

As if by one mind our little group does a Texas sidestep until there's only a big wet empty space where we've been standing. Perhaps a bell captain signals, because a waiter swiftly materializes and with two strong swipes of a napkin removes the urine from the floor, and moves on with hardly a pause. Clearly, Louella is known at the Beverly Wilshire.

Deftly, Sam takes my place at Louella's elbow, dismissing me with a curt nod. I've served my purpose as a young date for Louella. Making excuses to Sheree I slip away in my tux with its red cummerbund. There's still time to make it back to the Andalusia, maybe just to sit around and watch news clips of the Army–Joe McCarthy hearings on TV.

As I leave the ballroom Sam grabs my wrist and commands: "You say nothing, do nothing. Because it isn't happening."

I have seen the system up close—and it works.

❖

ALL ACROSS AMERICA, in offices and factories, there exists a "clearance procedure" in which a person suspected of treason may purge himself by confessing to sin, any sin, it doesn't matter if it's true or not just that you confess.

ONCE A VICTIM, now I'm an accomplice.

33

A Perfect Crime

"SAY GOODBYE TO your virginity, Kid. You're about to lose it."

Today is *tuchus oifen dem tisch* time. Mary needs my hands dirty. It must be like getting inducted into the Mafia: you have to kill somebody to prove that you are a man of honor.

Mary Baker and I are partners in crime at the comfortable Beverly Hills office of Martin Gang, the lawyer of choice for the purification ceremony of "clearance." Four exceedingly strange men supervise this informer-based blacklist operation that rules my Hollywood: lawyer Gang; Roy Brewer, the Nero-like stagehands union leader whose thumbs-up or -down dictates who lives or dies on the job; William Wheeler, the amiable, star-struck investigator for the House Un-American Committee; and a shadowy "progressive" psychotherapist who specializes in turning his patients into informers.

Martin Gang is a prominent rainmaker, *consigliere* to the stars, the Jewish establishment's point man in scrubbing (for a fee) the stain of disloyalty from Hollywood personalities. He operates under a strategy that correctly perceives the Red Scare as driven by anti-Semitism; he and his brother *balabatim* have made a tribal decision to oppose the witch hunt by cooperating with congressional Jew-baiters who call famous movie actors by their Yiddish birth names (Emanuel Goldenberg, Jules Garfinkle, Bernie Schwartz, Sam Klausman, etc.) as if this is prima facie proof of treason. HUAC member Rep. John Rankin curses them on the House floor as "Communist kikes."

Probably like Rabbi Magnin, Gang sees his religious duty as sacrificing a Jew to save a Jew, a medieval German tradition updated by the Nazis in the "bloodlands" of wartime Poland and Russia where the Judenrat, the Jewish self-police, on threat of death, were forced to organize the deportation of other Jews to the murder camps.

You do what you can or must to save a brother Jew. Except that this is America and no Nazi is holding a gun to lawyer Gang's head.

And our client today isn't Jewish.

He's "Chris McCoy," an accomplished screenwriter of westerns and thrillers, his quote a lovely $1,250 a week. Chris is a tall, gangly Westerner like the cowboys he writes about except that no cowhand gets into the kind of trouble he's in today. Martin Gang is our hired gun to watch Chris's back against the Clanton gang in Washington, DC.

On the drive over in Mary's Cadillac DeVille convertible (Chanel red to match her lipstick) I drum up the nerve,
finally, to ask her why, if the agency ran into such trouble
over its leftish clients, they hired me?

Mary sighs: "Institutional guilt, if you must know. When
the subpoenas started flying, we didn't lift a finger to protect
our clients. You're our sacrifice to the gods."

She looks over at me with one of her spectacular smiles.
"But you gotta earn it, Kid. Like today."

The lawyer's penthouse office has wraparound Polaroid
windows that automatically darken with the sun and, it
seems, our mood.

Martin Gang, warm and friendly, a chunky man with
curly hair, comes around his paperless desk to shake hands
with Chris McCoy, who has been waiting for us, and gives
Mary a big hug. "Hel-lo, sweetheart, how are the girls?"

Mary is a mother?

He turns to the tall, taciturn screenwriter: "Chris. 'Are
you now or have you ever been . . . ?'" He wants us to know
he's in on the joke.

But Chris is a serious guy. "No," he says.

"What?"

"No, never," repeats Chris.

"But your wife—" Gang is thrown off balance, he didn't
want to get down to business so fast.

"Look," Gang gestures, "shall we all sit down? The
couch there. I'll take the doctor's chair, ha ha." He draws

up an Eames aluminum executive chair, a throne-like affair, to face us. Chris takes a straightback chair in the corner, isolated, farther away from Mary and me sitting side by side, as if for mutual protection or aggression, on the leather settee.

Chris stubbornly: "No, never. I didn't go to meetings or sign anything."

Gang purses his lips and tents his fingers, thoughtfully. "That," he decides, "is unfortunate."

"What?"

"You must have done something to get on a List."

"Sorry."

"You have nothing to confess?"

"That's right. I've done nothing wrong."

"Please listen," Gang leans in intently. "The only way to help yourself is, you must confess to something. It just looks so evasive . . . sinister . . . if you don't."

Gang rises to go behind his desk, chooses a key on his keychain to unlock a metal file drawer, and pulls out a stapled, brass-bound sheaf of papers. "Boilerplate," he smiles again, apologetically, and comes back to us in the doctor-patient intimacy. He reaches over to delicately deposit the papers on Chris's lap. "Just fill in the blanks. A formality. We do the rest."

Chris flips through the pages and reads aloud at random: "'As an impressionable youth I cried when I saw unemployed war veterans selling apples on the street corner. The Communists took advantage of my youth. I was a dupe . . .'" Almost word for word what Bubbles Kahane asked me to sign at Columbia Pictures. They make no adjustments for age and gender. Just sign and be done with it. Outwardly, I'm cool and calm. It's just how the business is done. But inside, a raging self-contempt barely under control.

❖

MARY: "WHOEVER WRITES this stuff, Marty, tell him not to give up his day job. Jesus!"

Chris inquires, "Do all your clients agree to this?"

Gang says, "Of course we adjust to family circumstances. For example, you're married to the writer 'Tricia Singer'—"

"Leave her out."

Gang shifts an impatient gaze to Mary. Back to Chris. "Impossible. Since you say you were not a Party member and she is—"

"How do you know?" Chris snaps.

Gang's look at Mary says, We all know why we're here. I'm losing patience.

"Do you understand, Chris," he lectures, "how complicated it was to arrive at this point with you? God willing, trust me, you should never have such problems writing a script for Zanuck. Incidentally, I love your pictures." He goes on. "There's a whole industry. Predatory tabloids like 'Aware', 'Counterattack', 'Red Channels', and the Catholic Legion of Decency, you can't imagine how much they charge for a private consultation, the theatrical unions, Roy Brewer . . ."

Chris looks surprised. "They all look at . . . this piece of paper?"

"Absolutely."

"But it's all a lie. They'd be crazy to believe it."

"That's where I come in. And Congressman Nixon. And his investigator here in town, our man Wheeler. They're zealots."

"Is that why I'm paying you so much money?"

"My fee is modest. The rest is . . ." Gang shrugs. Why is Chris McCoy being such a hardass?

"Your wife is the key. We know all about her."

"Who is 'we'?"

"I've seen her FBI dossier."

"She died ten years ago."

Gang is surprised. Someone screwed up. "Ah, I'm sorry. I must have missed that. That's the other problem. She's deceased and cannot recant."

❖

CHRIS MCCOY'S CRAGGY face reflects the emotions I dare not show, or even feel: shame, anger, impotent rage. Don't shuck it, Clancy. You've come this far. *You do what you must.*

Chris and Gang lock eyes. Does Marty know how close he is to being beaten to death on his own Afghan carpet? Maybe he does. Gang's voice softens low and compassionate.

"I'm sorry to tell you, Chris, but Mrs. McCoy, *avisholem*," pause, looks down, "may her memory be for a blessing," pause with nodding of head, "God bless her, she's the reason you're in this room."

Later, when it's all signed and sealed, and Chris, silent and ashen, has gone his way, Mary and I are alone in her office overlooking Sunset Strip drinking straight Wyborowa vodka from her well-stocked fridge.

"Your first blood, Clancy. Rite of passage. How does that make you feel?" Mary asks.

"Sorry for Chris McCoy. He really got jammed."

"No, I mean how do you feel? Could you do it again? We've got more clients who need a washup."

"I'll pass."

"No, you won't. Either in or out."

"Somebody should shoot Martin Gang," I say.

"I'm an ace duck hunter," Mary says. "Last time I was in London I bought a Purdey over-and-under on Audley Street you wouldn't believe what they charged me. If you killed Marty, the line would be a mile long to fill his shoes." Pause. "We can shoot him later. After our business with him is done. If it ever is."

We. We'll shoot. Her erotic force field is like a bridle on me.

She removes her slouch hat and shakes her hair loose. Another secret: unbound, it falls to her shoulders, like Dorothy Malone, the rare book clerk in Bogart's *The Big Sleep*. And my mother Jennie.

"Well?"

"How many times will you make me do this?" I ask.

"What? Get raped?" She gives that throaty laugh that excites me. I've had three vodkas. "Again, and again . . . and again."

She empties the cobalt cocktail shaker into both our glasses.

"Want to come to England with me?"

"You giving up the business?"

"It's a thought. Especially on days like this."

We exchange hard-agent looks.

"What are your terms?" I ask.

She gets up and straightens the gray suit on her slim athletic body.

"To be negotiated," she murmurs.

❖

MARY SAYS THERE'S no turning back.

Every day my fever rises a little more about her. Now that we're partners in crime, anything is possible. I can't stop thinking about her.

Or my mother Jennie.

34

Portrait of Jennie

Jennifer Jones (as Jennie): I know we were meant to be together. The strands of our lives are woven together and neither the world nor time can tear them apart.

—*Portrait of Jennie* (1948), a David Selznick production. Leonardo Bercovici, who adapted original story, will be blacklisted.

"SAY THERE WAITRESS, shake a leg! Faster service over here!" My fist hammers the Formica counter.

The woman in a floral apron at the sandwich griddle has her back to me, flipping over a burger patty for the only other customer at this fast-food concession in a grocery market in Hawthorne in Southwest LA, not far from the ocean and El Segundo and its Douglas aircraft plant. The lone patron is a Douglas mechanic wearing overalls.

"Come on, baby," I hassle, "let's see some movement there." The guy at the end stool growls, "Take it easy, sonny, you'll last longer."

The waitress slaps his burger down, then comes over to lean on the counter close enough for me to catch the scent of her Max Factor Hypnotique. "What'll you have, big fella?"

The guy gawps. I tell him, "She's my ma."

"Kids today," he says.

Jennie and I like to pretend I'm hitting on her, a joke, I hope. She runs this hash joint as a life-saver after Catalina Swimwear laid off workers like her to retool for a new fashion season. She's her own boss and the nearly bankrupt market owner likes how she brings in the few customers who hang around to shoot the breeze and buy stuff. It can't be her cooking, there are just so many ways to mangle a toasted cheese sandwich.

"What's your secret, Ma?"

Simply: "Me."

So that's where I get it.

We share the love that dare not speak its name . . . mother and son, too near and too far apart, too hot not to cool down. When we're alone, the lone customer sloping off with a dime tip, Ma does her Rita Hayworth-as-Gilda bit, swinging her ample hips and flipping up and tumbling her hair down around her shoulders, hair no longer flame-red but almost all gray, and rough puckered arms, slippered feet. Don't let yourself go, Ma. Gilda's boyfriend Glenn Ford won't like it.

We stay away from each other out of overwhelming need. Except for times when I fill in as her short-order cook—my habit is to come around, like Cagney's psycopath killer Cody Jarrett in *White Heat*, when I need my mother's absolution for a crime as yet uncommitted. The **nine names** in my wallet.

"So . . . what's new?" She lights up her usual Pall Mall and matches it in a regal Mary Baker gesture, sizing me up. For just an instant she is Mrs. Baker.

"Ma, I got this new job."

"Wear a tie maybe? That last job you smelled of bananas a mile away."

I'm a talent and literary agent, I tell her.

Her eyes light up. "A business agent—which union?" Jennie and my dad were labor organizers.

I brag, "I have an expense account at Romanoff's and Perino's. Humphrey Bogart knows me. Mary Astor and Joseph Cotton are on my list." Astor is Jennie's favorite movie slut, the faithless Brigid O'Shaughnessy in *The Maltese Falcon*. When I was a kid, Ma, shocked but savoring, read aloud from tabloid coverage of Astor's child-custody trial where her sex diary, including the orgasms, was entered in evidence. ("Oh, so many exquisite moments—twenty, count them diary, twenty!")

"Bogart," Ma sniffs. "A cruel mouth. I read such guys like a book. No wonder Mayo Methot threw him out." She swears she never spends a penny on the gossip mags but somehow is always up on the latest.

"You're out of date, Ma. He's with Lauren Bacall."

"Jewish girl," Ma says. "Go do likewise."

She won't give up, craves for me to have a loving partner missing from her own life, wants a grandchild and at this point almost doesn't care from whom. On my last visit she suggested I stick a pin in my rubber "or whatever you use."

"Diaphragms. That's what women do."

"Diagrams? Some help."

"Ma, you shouldn't live alone. You sound like Mollie Goldberg on her TV show," which featured Philip Loeb playing the father until he killed himself after being named by Elia Kazan and my client Lee J. Cobb.

Ma says, "Cobb is wonderful in *Call Northside 777*. He helps Jimmy Stewart save an innocent man from jail."

I say, "Stewart plays FBI agents now."

"Good casting."

"Ma . . . ?" She knows I'm asking about the Federal badges who are pressuring her to pressure me.

She turns to clean the fry top, scrubs and scrapes, puts her heart into it.

"You let them in?"

"I serve Van de Kamp cookies with milk and read Emma Goldman to them."

"They must love that."

"They must love something. I see more of them than I do of you." The feebs harass Ma because of me, and me partly because of her.

She reaches over the counter to affectionately rub my buzz cut. "It's too short."

She looks at me with infinite sadness. "Sometimes, the way you live, no roots, nobody to care for you, I feel like John Dillinger's mother, always thinking, you're dead or in jail or waiting for some Lady in Red to bring you down. All your girlfriends! Which one is your Lady in Red?"

"Ma," I blurt, reaching across to kiss her cheek, "come live with me. I'll apply for that veteran's loan and we'll buy that house in the Valley you always wanted. And you can grow roses."

She sighs. "I've waited so long to hear you say that." She gives a little despairing laugh. "It would kill us both, Kalman." She uses my Yiddish name, an unusual intimacy.

We both know how it will end, so what we do, in loving evasion, is launch into this song and dance, humming the melody of "The Lady in Red," Xavier Cugat version cha-cha, and I hold out my arms which, laughing, she can't resist, and glancing to see if anyone's watching she comes around the counter and together, in the almost empty food market, warbling a capella as we dance and sway, to words I reinvented as:

"Oh! The lady with red hair
The fellas are all crazy
For the lady with red hair
She's a big gaudy
But naudy
What a personality . . ."

❖

FREE THINKING AS she sees herself, Jennie is slightly ashamed of finding sneaky ways to check if any of the women I'm seeing are Jewish. "Not that I care . . . but . . ."

"My boss is teaching me Yiddish."

"She's Jewish?"

"The opposite."

"Tell her she's doing me a *toiveh*."

"She likes Jews. Says they saved her life."

"Lucky her. If you know who they are, send them around to me."

"You always have me, Ma."

"That's my problem."

35

Torah! Torah! Torah!

*The greatest danger to this country lies in (the Jews')
large ownership and influence of motion pictures.*

—American flying hero Colonel Charles Lindbergh

Relief for the Jews? What I need is relief from the Jews!

—Columbia Pictures boss Harry Cohn, himself Jewish, on being
asked to contribute to a Jewish charity

T HE MONDAY AFTER Bogie's premiere party I walk
into a shitstorm of my own making. Keep in mind, I
was hired because I'm the youngest agent so must have my
finger on the pulse of the growing youth audience. Right.

❖

SCENE 1: FILM DIRECTOR Nicholas Ray's Warner
Brothers office in Burbank. He is casting *Rebel Without a
Cause*, which studio boss Jack Warner hates as a subver-
sion of "American values." Under studio pressure to get a

finished script or abandon ship, Nick Ray hesitates because he can't decide who should play his lead Jim Stark. Nick likes me, ever since I found him a young and almost untried writer, Stewart Stern, to solve the difficult story when more experienced screenwriters had failed. Another reason Nick trusts me is that we have subtly signaled our dirty pasts to each other, two survivors who dodged the bullet. Now he begs me to be his "other pair of eyes" sizing up a certain young Method actor waiting in his outer office. As a personal favor, please?

The moment I enter, the boy places his bare, dirty feet on the desk and defiantly buries his nose in a book. Sullen, he's in raggedy jeans and a filthy T-shirt in contrast to my own uniform of wide-lapel navy pinstripe double-breasted three-piece suit with vest, Harvey & Hudson button-down linen double-cuff dress shirt, mother-of-pearl CS initialed cufflinks, lavender-blue Bulgari tie, crew-top haircut. The new kid's contemptuous glance tells me where in his universe I stand: below nowhere. It's impossible to strike up a chat with this cave boy, he's like a Cro-Magnon dug up from a Paleolithic site with grunts and inaudible mutters and a half smile like a Parkinson tic, and even at this distance I can sniff his body odor. He refuses to look directly at me but at the walls, the ceiling, Alpha Centauri. So much for my agent's charm.

"Well?" asks Nick Ray anxiously. The kid, I report, is monosyllabic, possibly retarded, and needs a bath. "A director's nightmare. Forget him."

❖

Scene 2: A few days later. Sam Jaffe's ground-floor office on Sunset Strip, where he solicits my advice on an eighteen-year-old Mississippi country singer billed as "The Hillbilly Cat" whose manager is looking for a Hollywood agent to make the boy a movie star. Mr. Jaffe says, "Be honest, tell me what you think of this kid, Perry Como he's not." He draws the drapes to set up a 16mm projector for a grainy kinescope tape—Sam refuses to have a TV in his life. What I see on the screen is a grease ball who masturbates his guitar and sneers the blues through his nose.

"Clancy, it's your call, he's available, sign him or not?"

"He can't carry a tune, they'll hate him in the big cities, and a movie star? Please! Pass."

I've just rejected James Dean and Elvis Presley as clients.

Mary summons me to her office.

"You've just cost the agency half a million in commissions," her first words, calmly.

"You firing me?" I ask.

She's surprisingly affable. "You're such a drama queen. Come over here, Kid, and have a drink." She sets it up on her desk, a bottle of A.A. Hirsch Reserve bourbon, leave her to drink a whiskey I've never heard of. We tip glasses. "*L'Chaim*," she toasts.

She looks at me through her glass as if assessing me anew. After a long pause she decides. "Clancy, we're agents, not Nostradamus." Another sip. "It's happened to better men. Like me. I almost signed Ava Gardner but all I saw was thick ankles and redneck accent. Monty Clift? Just another neurotic *feigelah*." She notes my anxiety. "Relax. Try sex."

She called me by name, not "Kid." Does she feel something for me?

The strange thing about the Jaffe office is that while we're all competitive with each other as well as with rival agents, none of the platoon takes advantage of my screwup to stick in the knife even though my misjudgments take a bite out of their year-end bonus. Instead, they seem to view my stupidity almost like a war wound, just got unlucky is all. That is, except the ever-reliable Jonny Buck who pops his head in my office to grin, "Elvis Presley AND James Dean. Im-press-ive." But Zack Silver, like most of us already booze-buzzed by 10 A.M., simply waves away my blunders. "C'mon, it's only money. Have one on me." There's hardly a Jaffe agent who doesn't have a bottle (or two) in his bottom desk drawer; Mary shamelessly brings her own unlabeled rye to restaurants, yet I've never, not once, seen any of us drunk on duty. Pissed out of our minds, but high functioning.

I'm the only doper agent, on Tuinal, Seconal, Miltown, asthma inhalers, Benzies, Dexxies, whatever's going aside from Ray Kovacs's coke which makes me sneeze. "How can you take that shit?" Jonathan Buck, a four-martini man and a huge smoker, demands as he watches me swallow a clump of reds to pump me up for studio calls. Almost all the agents and secretaries pop trankies called Miltown, so they should talk.

Boozing is part of the Jaffe value system. (Mary: "I don't trust anyone who's not an alcoholic.") Fall-down drunks Sam would never tolerate; however, sex is built into the office mosaic. Impossible to track who is sleeping with whom, agents with secretaries, the only way to note is who stays after hours and what woman in the midst of taking dictation bursts into tears with the agent hastily closing the door. Everybody seems to be doing it aside from Mary Baker—what's her deal?—and Addy-with-a-y who, having once taken care of me in the storage room, has her hands full with a troubled teenage son and then, of course, there is my receptionist Joanna, the Orthodox rabbi's daughter.

Joanna is young, single, bursting out of her blouse, and wears a curly wig.

"But a wig is only for married Jewish women." I know that much.

"I'm almost married," Joanna retorts. "I'm engaged. To a finer boy than you'll ever be."

I've never made it with a baldheaded lady. "And you never will," Joanna informs me. "Unless you convert."

"Convert? I am a Jew."

"Ha!"

"Want to see?"

"You're disgusting."

"I'll go ultra-Orthodox."

"It takes years. You'll do the *kabbalatal mitzvoth?* The *mikveh?* Live pure?"

"Whatever it takes."

"You have no god."

"There. You said it! You're not supposed to."

"I hate you. You'll make me a bad Jew but I can't make you a good Jew."

"Don't cry, Joanna. Only kidding around."

"Like hell."

"Jews don't believe in hell."

❖

THAT EVENING, AS I'm leaving the office, Mary's assistant Cricket calls me back to Mary's office and shuts the door discreetly, leaving Mary alone with me.

Mary, thoughtfully: "You've made yourself vulnerable with this latest can of worms. Start going to temple. It looks good on your FBI file."

She knows! Has known all this time!

But temple?

"Some Jew," she scoffs. "*Ich bin a besser yid als due.*" (I'm a better Jew than you.)

She lays it out. As a result of FBI visits to Sam and Phil Gersh, and negative gossip from Jaffe relatives, and because Sam's family is upset I'm flirting with his two grown daughters, I'm due for the chop. "And now Billy is on our *toochis.*"

Billy Wilder?

No, Billy Wilkerson, owner-editor of the influential trade rag *The Hollywood Reporter*, a Mobbed-up blackmailer and drinkin' buddy of J. Edgar Hoover. Wilkerson practically invented the industry-enforced blacklist with his front page editorial:

> *Any man or woman who, under the guise of freedom of speech, or the cloak of the Bill of Rights, or under the pseudo protection of being a liberal, says things, causes*

things to be said, or who actually is involved with many
of the conspiracies that have now infested this great
land of ours, has no place among us, be he commie or
what. He or she should be rushed out of our business.

❖

SAM JAFFE LOATHES Wilkinson as a night crawling crud
but also fears his malignancy.

Mrs. Baker draws a breath. "*Gayn shul.* Do us a favor.
Make respectable. Then come back and do overtime to bring
in new clients to make up for your shortfall. *Gai arois, boy-*
chik, und gevein a goniff." (Go out there, young man, and
rob somebody.)

I love the robbing part.

As instructed, yarmulke and conservative suit, I attend
synagogue for the first time in my life, on Wilshire Boulevard
near the Brown Derby, at Rabbi Edgar Magnin's magnificent gothic-Byzantine "temple to the Hollywood stars," a
Christian church in all but name.

Pulling open its King Kong–sized doors is like walking
into an ornate Balaban & Katz movie theater, its pseudo-
13th-century stained glass and hundred-foot-long bib-
lical wall murals commissioned by Jack Warner (who
like most Jewish moguls has a shikseh wife). The Second
Commandment may mandate no graven images but what
the *Gehenna*, this is Los Angeles, what a contrast between
Magnin's gold-plated splendor and the shabby little shuls of
my old Chicago neighborhood.

"AND SO?" MARY asks the following Monday.

Truth is, in Rabbi Magnin's Wilshire temple I mostly craned my neck scouting for business. Worse, while chanting along with the *Shema* and *Bracha* blessing, I kept staring at the Torah in the Ark thinking, Is there a movie in it? Of course! *Samson and Delilah* made a mint.

"Otherwise . . . nothing. Nada. God did not speak to me. But after services I pitched a couple of stories outside on the steps."

Now is not the time to raise the delicate matter of Rabbi Magnin who, like most of the industry's leading Jews, caved to the blacklist anti-semites. It's hard to listen to a rabbi with sex appeal but no guts.

Do Jews, like Christians, believe in miracles? From Mary and Sam I seem to be contracting a strange contagion— *kashrut*. Over time they're restoring in me a denied, or forgotten, if ever known, link to those shabby 16th Street shuls I grew up among and for whose davening congregants I was a "Shabbas goy," the kid who got a nickel for switching on the electric bulb often followed by a slap across the mouth for desecrating the Sabbath.

Kashrut. Jaffe has his own way of translating this ancient, Talmud-based dietary law into his business practice. As done by Sam it's an expression of Yiddishkeit, "Jewishness," is it kosher, fair, legitimate, right? He'll break off in the middle of his Tuesday staff inspirationals to implore us to work longer, pitch harder, be more aggressive, knock on more doors, make more phone calls, steal more clients—then he'll raise a cautionary finger, "But be mensch. Kick the other guy to the curb—but don't run him over."

Kashrut. Kosher.

Like the US Constitution the Talmud could use a little updating . . .

. . . One of my writer clients, "Dorothy Dunstable," needs a job because—she doesn't know this yet—but I do—that her husband is about to drop a dime on her by testifying that she has, or may have had, or perhaps still has, as a patriotic American he thought the House Committee should know, "Communist connections."

Normally I'd never dream of pitching a client to producer William Alland at Universal who as a HUAC "friendly witness" informs on his own writers, a Jack Warner trick. I want his business but why put my clients' heads in his noose? Yet a baser instinct tells me Dorothy Dunstable and Alland just might click. Dorothy, an attractive, shy, nervous New Yorker writer and I stroll over to Alland's bungalow while I brief her about him. I am especially fond of her because she worked on a thriller that was the first Hollywood film to show actual footage of the Nazi death camps; in my book that makes her a hero. Alland's office is deserted for lunch so we dawdle in the waiting room. His appointment book lies open on his secretary's desk where a glance reveals that he has two appointments ahead of us from rival agents so, naturally, with my new Waterman gold-filigree-overlay fountain pen I neatly scratch in Dorothy's name above the other names. When the secretary returns she glances at her book and ushers Dorothy and me into Alland's office as he returns from the commissary. Upshot, Dorothy gets the job on a ten-week guarantee after I "mistakenly" raise her quote by another $250 a week. And almost exactly ten weeks later, her husband slips into executive session to testify against her. But by then she's salted away enough money for lawyers. And a divorce.

Kashrut. It depends on how you translate it. The sequel. Screenwriter Stewart Stern, a brilliant and sensitive young ex-GI who fought at the Battle of the Bulge, has scored with his script for Nick Ray's *Rebel Without a Cause*, succeeding where a string of higher-priced A-list writers failed. He got the assignment when James Dean met and liked Stewart's large heart and modest manner, so different from mine.

Now is my time to shine at the negotiating table. We're in the big conference room at Warners.

"What's his quote?" asks Bill Dozier, the studio second-in-command. Stewart almost blurts out his true poverty wage that he got on his last job when I kick him under the table.

❖

"TWELVE FIFTY ON a fifteen-week guarantee," I testify, my eyes sparkling with honesty.

Nick Ray, the director, knows I'm lying but is mute.

Dozier laughs, "Come on, Clancy!"

Stewart, not wanting to lose his first big credit, opens his mouth to speak again—such an honest boy! Under the table I kick his leg really hard.

A sweaty hour later, a deal is consummated, at $1,250 on a ten-week guarantee.

Just as we're breaking up with handshakes all around: Jack Warner himself, all trim mustache and check sports jacket, master of all he surveys, strolls in, and Dozier reports the deal. Warner's mouth tightens as he crooks his trigger finger at me, and outside in the corridor crowds me against a wall where he positively fire-breathes after-shave. For a split second I think he's nailed me politically.

THANK HEAVEN, HE only has money on his mind.

"Twelve fifty! Twelve fifty!" he screeches dementedly. Is he going to hit me? "What am I, a *freier* just in from Youngstown, Ohio? Next time you rob me put a mask on your fucking face and do it with a gun. You are one lucky kike. I've sunk so much money into this sonofabitching bastard, I can't afford to hire any more writers."

The effort of keeping his temper—this is his idea of restraint?—is too much. He grabs the lapel of my herringbone jacket. Fiercely, in my face: "Shylock! *Putz! Putz goniff! Bluz in toches! Franzen zol esn zany laybe! KHAZER!!*" Bile pours out of his system, such a contrast with his Waspy sportif look.

Jack Warner subsides as quickly as he erupts, then pushes me off as he straightens out his clothes. He actually smiles as he pats my shoulder.

"But *kluge*," he says admiringly. (Clever.) "*Tsair kluge.*" (Very clever.) And struts away almost as if he has put something over on me.

P.S. Stewart Stern does a superb job on *Rebel*, earning every penny of the quote I lied for.

36

The Informer

Vitctor McLaglen (as Gypo Nolan): 'Twas I informed on your son, Mrs. McPhillip. Forgive me.

Una O'Connor (as Mrs. McPhillip): Ah, Gypo, I forgive you. You didn't know what you were doing.

Vitctor McLaglen: Frankie! Frankie! Your mother forgives me!

—Dying words of the betrayer in John Ford's *The Informer* (1935)

I NFORMERS RULE MY Hollywood.

The old rule was "Nothing happens without a script first." Today nothing happens without a person of talent tattling on his best friend. Nobody is innocent. You squeal to survive, which is why, for insurance purposes, I keep those **names** primed, locked, and loaded.

Meanwhile, down there, on the ocean floor, among the tube worms and deep sea creatures, is arch-informer William Alland, my buddy, benefactor, pal, friend, and patron—and probably betrayer—who has mentored, welcomed, and made me feel comfortable at home in his home, sprawling Universal Pictures—the oldest Valley studio.

Bill Alland makes very profitable low-to-medium budget horror, western, and sci-fi pictures, and hence is a consummate potential buyer of Jaffe Agency writers, actors, and material. From the moment I snuck onto the lot to peddle my goods, Alland has gone out of his way to charm, tease, befriend, and seduce me. In his bungalow office he patiently listens to my pitches, laughs at my jokes—and is aware I avoid selling him writers because he named names including screenwriters he had personally hired (also his ex-wife). Early in my agency tenure I'd strut past his office with my nose in the air, and he'd come out on his verandah and cheerfully call out, "Hey, Agent Man! I make more product than anyone else on this lot. Deal with it!" And he'd wave me in, like a maitre d'.

"I know who you are," he leans back in his leatherette chair, "and you know what I am. So let's cut the shit." Shamefully, I'm grateful for his hand of friendship because most other Universal producers I barge into—Al Zugsmith, Aaron Rosenberg, Howard Christie, Albert Cohen, Robert Arthur—are old-school tough and mouths to match. ("Agents know shit. You are shit. Ignoramuses on parade. Fuck off, and next time you come through the door have something to say!") Despite my own style, borrowed from Kirk Douglas in his crueler moments (see *Ace in the Hole* and *The Champion*), I'm physically afraid of Rosenberg, a former USC All-American famous for his vicious tackling; and Zugsmith who, gangster-hard, cigar in mouth, sounds more like Mickey Cohen than Cohen himself. Wandering around Universal and taking deep breaths before invading their offices, I feel very alone, on my own, for myself only, ambition my only solace.

Bill Alland is a small, sharp-faced, pockmarked man with a high-pitched but powerful tone that millions remember, even if they don't know his name, as the God-like Voice of the *March of Time*–style newsreel in Orson Welles's *Citizen Kane*, where he also plays Reporter Thompson, whose on-camera interviews shape the narrative of "the greatest movie ever made." Automatically that puts him in my movie pantheon.

So I have to wonder, as I sit across from him, does Alland ever think about his scene in *Kane* where as a reporter he interrogates the drunken actress Dorothy Comingore who plays Charles Foster Kane's operatic mistress? Bill Alland prospered after he testified, but Comingore suffered a career-ending blacklist when her husband, Paul Jarrico's writing partner Richard Collins, nailed her and grabbed custody of their son; she committed "suicide on the installment plan" by becoming fatally alcoholic. Hitler had a habit of letting certain artists—Furtwängler, Gründgens, Riefenstahl, Richard Strauss—off the hook because in his eyes they were *gottbegnadet* or "divinely gifted." Simply because Alland performs a minor but critical role in a great movie, is he unaccountable as an artist?

Or is he just my bread and butter?

Alland is by nature a tantalizer, dropping serial hints that any day now he'll buy a script from me while almost in the same breath he happily and compulsively chatters on and on and on and on about his House Un-American testimony.

He's merely amused to learn I'm a friend of one of the writers he named.

"Ha, yes, Bernie Gordon! Used him—"

"You sure did!"

His face flushes only slightly. "Were you in the service? Yeah? What a surprise. I flew combat, took Jap ackack up my ass, Gordon and his pal Jarrico deserved what they got. Slackers. Didn't have the guts to enlist."

Wrong. Jarrico was in the wartime Merchant Marine and US Navy.

Alland, unhearing, "The Communists stayed home and hid in their swimming pools while I fought. End of story."

My dilemma is how to squeeze business out of Alland without totally shaming myself? Alland gets a big kick out of twisting me in the wind.

But then his anger will boil up in a sudden, raging acne from forehead to chin, so like mine after an FBI visit, when the born actor in him launches yet more allocutions of his serial betrayals. ("Is the world worse off because I forced a few mediocre writers to become decent carpenters and plumbers?")

He snarls, sobs, is alternately ice cold and hotly atoning, bragging, taunting and challenging, demanding I tell him what I would have done in his place, blames his present wife's extravagances for caging him in bad choices, only to claim in the next breath that he informed from purely patriotic motives. He even insists that his space-alien films are coded attacks on McCarthyism. "Oh yes?" I say, "my mistake, I thought they tell us that anyone who thinks, looks, and talks differently is a foreign life form bent on destroying our American Way of Life."

"Well," he grins, not taking offense, "it works both ways." Yes, why not?

He keeps his small black glittering eyes on me talking, talking, without buying, buying, while insisting that his gold-digging wife is the root of his evil, her greed, her insatiable demands for jewelry and cars.

Right. Put it on the wife. Good one, Bill.

I say, "Next you'll tell me the devil made you do it."

Impish grin. "Caught me, didn't you? Speaking of which, any new material for me?"

I toss a tear sheet from Zane Grey's *Western Magazine* on his desk. "Ah yes the devil, there's this gunslinger named Lucifer rides into a town called Hell, Wyoming and—" I make up this stuff all the time.

He's laughing. "Okay okay, you're vamping. Good show. How'd you ever become an agent anyway? Fall through the cracks?"

Got that right.

Weeks go by and he refuses to close a sale.

Little by little, over time, teasing is his game plan, he draws me into a labyrinth of friendship, even affection—he's hard not to like. And then, unasked for, one sunny day he surprises me with an offer of a paid apprenticeship under him: to watch him at work, look over his shoulder in the editing room, learn how to add up a production budget. "If you're good, I'll give you a credit," he promises. Uh huh. Will I have to be cleared? "Not by me," he says, "but by the studio." A Faustian deal. Somehow Bill's X-ray eye, plucked from the bleeding socket of one of his sci-fi aliens, sees straight into my back pocket with the **nine names**. I'm hungry for it.

CLANCY SIGAL ASSISTANT TO THE PRODUCER

CLANCY SIGAL EXECUTIVE PRODUCER

A CLANCY SIGAL PICTURE

He's such a sadist.

But before I can jump . . .

There comes a day like this:

"What I'm looking for," his opening gambit, "is a futuristic story about a human monster born without a conscience but who we feel sorry for at the end even though he's wrecked a whole city. The kicker is, he can change ordinary citizens into monsters like himself just by looking at them. Got anything like it in your bag of tricks?"

I ask, "Are you going to call it *The William Alland Story?*"

Stung, he leaps from his chair and comes around the desk, and falls to his knees to grab both my hands in his. My flesh crawls.

"*'Twas I informed on your son, Mrs. McPhillip,*" Bill Alland weeps. "*Forgive me.*" He's mimicking the last lines of John Ford's tragic movie. Bill's voice ventriloquizes up high to that of the grieving mother. "*Ah, Gypo, I forgive you. You didn't know what you were doing.*" Bill-as-Gypo looks heavenward, and, just before dying, pleads to God, "*Frankie! Frankie! Your mother forgives me!*"

And goes full-length prostrate on the floor like a penitent. Jaysus, what an act.

On my own knees I peer closely at his pitted face. Those are real tears. He pokes his head up and grins, gets up off the floor, and wipes the sweat from his small round face with a handkerchief.

I put my hands together and clap. "Bill," I ask, "do you never feel guilty about anything at all?"

He gives a short laugh and returns to his chair. "Remorse? Well, yes. That I didn't fire the director on my last picture before he went over budget. Now that's guilt."

❖

P.S.: BLACKLISTED PAUL Jarrico, who has been named so often he deserves a Lifetime Achievement Award, makes me a startling offer.

"Rat on me. It will give you credibility with the studios, with guys like Alland, and then you use it to sell my work under the table. Let's not be martyrs. I'm broke. How about it?"

He doesn't know he is one of the **names** in my wallet.

Fyodor Dostoyevsky would love it: Bill Alland, the informer, and Paul Jarrico, the informed upon, are the two most guilt-free people I know in Hollywood.

❖

What's the difference between a good buddy and a "good German"?

In lawyer Gang's office I'm a good German because I'd had lots of practice.

HERMANN GOERING'S BALEFUL eye followed me clean out the door on my last day as a failed-assassin at his Nuremberg trial. Even on his way to the gallows, Goering had power over me in the same way he'd intimidated his fellow criminals.

SCHEISS JUDEN IST *nicht soldat.* The Jew is no soldier.

Now it's my turn to be like him.

I'm back in my former SS barracks in Frankfurt-am-Main, having blundered in my personal *nokmim,* a revenge mission to avenge Jewish blood, my only satisfaction being that I heard about the "Executioners' Unit" of partisan Jews who survived the murder camps and snuck into Occupied Germany to inject lethal doses of arsenic into loaves of bread intended for the SS-killer POWs at the Langwasser internment camp near Nuremberg. Hooray for Abba Kovner and his Jewish Brigade who succeeded where I failed! But back home in Frankfurt I'm reverting to just another drunken American dealing black market and bargaining sex with Fräuleins like my girlfriend Rita, a former anti-aircraft gunner in a Volksturm battery and the only honest woman I've met in all of Germany, who shrugs, "*Bestimmt,* of course I was Nazi. A believer. To the end. All those others—" she spits on the sidewalk—"*Lugner und Pfuscher* those *Furze.*"

Liars and farts. When I'm not with Rita I rooster about the pulverized city with a .45 back on my hip daring any German man, amputee or not, to look me in the eye. Big hero.

My barracks room is shared with "Orville Hudson," an overweight Warrant Officer whose hobby is smuggling German girls into his bed after CQ check in exchange for a bar of GI soap or pack of Chesterfields. One day Hudson persuades me to ride shotgun as he slips outside the wire for a rendezvous. Since she has brothers, I bring a weapon, chamber a round in the snout, and follow him downstairs into the bushes outside the Kaserne where, his trousers down to his ankles, he's fiercely shagging a small-boned German woman with her skirt up around her throat. Across the street two hulking German youths in shabby Wehrmacht uniforms watch. One of them leans on a crutch. They might be Werewolf die-hards, rumored to assassinate GIs, so I'm glad I brought the .45, but these guys have more of an exhausted than a dangerous look.

"Hey, help me out!" Hudson calls to me over his shoulder.

A closer look, she's a child of maybe eleven or twelve under Hudson.

"Get off her," I say.

"Wait your turn!" he laughs while humping and plunging.

I pull the .45 from my Ike jacket and put it right up against his ear. Hudson couldn't care less, but the pale bony German girl looks terribly frightened. I, not Hudson, am her enemy as I nudge him with the toe of my boot, then kick him hard in the ribs, but he still won't roll off her. She protectively tightens her grip around him.

Standing over both of them, piece in hand, I am para-
lyzed and stupid. An American soldier is raping, with or
without her consent, a child.

Her brothers across the street don't move.

I do nothing because he's my GI buddy and we're in a
foreign land.

Nothing. *Nicht mehr.*

❖

MARY BAKER AND I are firmly, intimately bonded as co-
conspirators. Thoughts of her consume me. Except for my
mother I've never had a crush on an older woman.

37

Picnic

W HEN MARY BAKER first interviewed me, the woman I saw across the Louis XIV desk was a middle-aged, hardnosed, take-no-prisoners business executive with a cigarette rasp and a mannish bearing and Bryn Mawr accent (like her classmate and sometime client Katharine Hepburn) I never hear raised in anger, which is unusual in a screaming Hollywood culture.

And then, surprising myself, I fall. And everyone knows it.

Cricket Kendall, Mary's protector and secretary—anything else going on between them?—with a toss of her head and cold glare signals that I'm vamping way above my pay grade.

Jonny Buck pauses by my office and with his OSS-trained eye looks me up and down and says, "She's married, you nut."

In the men's john Zack Silver, zipping up, mutters enigmatically, "Jennings Lang."

My brother agents all know it.

Worse, so does she.

This morning Mary intercoms me as usual, presumably as her go-to fireman to cool off another unhappy client. A simple matter of seduction. With restless screenwriters (a tautology) you praise and quote from their youthful novels they're proud of; directors you feed unsold scripts that will never be made just to keep them busy; actors you never praise early work because it ages them.

"*Tell all the truth/But at a slant . . .*" Emily Dickinson should have been an agent.

But when Mary calls me in, she asks Cricket to leave so it must be serious.

"Kid," Mary says (we're back to Kid?), leaning back in her chair, "Jennings Lang." That name again.

Normally, it's how we dance, she'll drop a name, a code word, which sends me off to hunt prey, spear in hand.

"What are Lang's credits?" I ask, as if I don't know.

She says, "Emergency surgery at St Luke's. He was our agent here and had an affair with a client, Joan Bennett, whose husband Walter Wanger shot his testicles off in the MCA parking lot."

Mary is informing me (a) she knows I'm nuts about her, and (b) I risk a bullet in the scrotum. But she hasn't said she doesn't care for me.

I'd love to lean over the desk and kiss that slash of Chanel lipstick off her.

She surprises me. "Come to my house tonight. The children are away skiing with their father."

"Black tie?" I joke.

Only once before, my first week on the job, I've been invited to Mary's Spanish Colonial Revival house on Roxbury Drive, a ritual obligation for any new employee. She lives just around the corner from Bugsy Siegel's mansion on Linden Drive where a sniper shot out his eyeball, which Mary believes may actually raise property values hereabouts. (It's rumored she won her house in a high-stakes poker game. What an Omega girl she'd make!) Still trailing a Connecticut country club sensibility, Mary had insisted on formal dress, in her dome-chandeliered dining room, its long table covered by a Battenburg hand-embroidered lace cloth, and of course dinnerware in Meissen. I kept a straight face when she tinkled a small silver bell to summon a black serving maid, whereupon she presided over dinner (squab under glass, eeew) of a dozen royal guests—Greg and wife, Ava and Frank, Doris and Marty, Joe and Rose Mankiewicz, etc.—with a sternly regal, unbending manner never seen in the office. Somewhere backstage she has a daughter or two and even a husband, it was said.

But tonight it's just us two.

"Just be on time," she had said. "But only after you make your last client calls."

At ten sharp—we work long days—I'm on Mary's doorstep with a bouquet of store-bought gladiolas. She, not her usual maid, answers the chimes (sounding the first bars of "A Fine Romance" from client Ginger Rogers's *Swing Time*) and leads me into her living room with tapestries on the wall and oil portraits of what I fear may be distant ancestors on horseback. For a Judeophile who glories in her adopted Yiddish culture, she certainly does have airs.

In front of the oversized couch is a picnic spread of roast chicken, ham, wine, and salad to which she gestures while she reclines on the rug-covered floor with the food-laden coffee table chaperoning us. Ah, Mary, even the coffee table linen is monogrammed two-hundred-year-old King of Prussia. Staring at us from the corner encased in a mahogany cabinet is a monster television set that must have cost a thousand bucks. (My own secondhand $15 tabletop b&w with rabbit ears I tossed into the garbage after watching Robert Young in *Father Knows Best* lead the family in prayer followed by a TV priest in ecclesiastical robes preach on "Life Is Worth Living.")

"Well," Mary says, arranging her tightly belted, orange-and-blue floor-length short-sleeve housecoat with a plunging neckline she wouldn't dream of exposing at the office, "here we are."

My heart is pumping. We're alone. I pretend to admire the tapestries, a wild mix of unicorns, Paris café scenes, Breughel peasants, and abstract design. Mary gives her low Barbara Stanwyck laugh. "Don't blame me, they came with the house. Doug Fairbanks had them as movie props." Fairbanks junior or senior? How old is Mary anyway?

Mary asks, "Would you be more comfortable if I came and sat beside you?"

I'm dying.

She does. Her scent, whatever it is, sends me nearly over the edge. It sure isn't Ma's Max Factor Hypnotique.

She relaxes by folding back her housecoat and placing her bare slim legs on the edge of the coffee table, and throws her head back, revealing a white throat that makes me feel like Dracula wanting to sink my fangs in.

She takes my hand. We haven't touched the food yet.

"Clancy . . ." Not kid. I'm home safe.

"Take me—or your Christmas bonus."

"What?" I withdraw my hand.

She looks deep into my eyes, "You have a death wish? Dating Phil Gersh's secretary who is Jack Dragna's personal property, what? And come on to both of Sam's daughters, which freaks out Sam's wife who considers you, not without reason, as white trash. Who are you, Forever Amber with balls, always sleeping upwards?" She gets that thoughtful look whenever her agent's mind clicks. "Speaking of which. *Forever Amber*. A Fox movie. We got commissions on Cornel Wilde and Ring Lardner for the screenplay. Oh, how we miss Ring, never out of work, two thousand a week, an Academy Award, he had it all the *schmegege*." Lardner, son of the famous sportswriter, is one of the Hollywood Ten and served nine months of a year sentence in the same prison as HUAC's chairman, J. Parnell Thomas, the extortionist Congressman who sent him there.

How can she be so practical in the midst of my romantic agony? Yet I'm so used to following the trail of her thinking that my own agent's mind automatically shifts to *Forever Amber* . . . Otto Preminger . . . Darryl Zanuck . . . Story: eighteenth-century whore sleeps her way into the king's bed. A flash image of my penis as an alien antenna from *The*

Thing from Another World groping, exploring, finding . . .
then electrocuted and going limp.

She pats my hand and lapses into her gentile Yiddish.

"*Nisht gefehlich*," she comforts me. Not so bad. "At
heart you're a *haymisheh tatellah*. But *ganzah fahrblunget*."
Nice, very young but crazy.

And then gives it to me straight. "Sam and I hired you
at great risk to the agency. We keep you on because you've
proved yourself. Despite. Phil thinks you're a Red—the
sooner we get rid of you the better. *The Hollywood Reporter*
threatens us over you. Even Sam's nephews call wanting to
know if we fired you yet. But you're still here. So, kid, let's
not spoil it."

❖

KID. I'M LOST.

She didn't invite me over to seduce but to punch me in
the mouth.

I'm embarrassed, angry, humiliated. Who asked her
to be old, married (where is he by the way, hiding behind
the drapes?), probably a lesbian and behave as if . . . as if
. . . what? I deeply resent her colonizing my mind, and am
ashamed for letting myself feel something for her.

On her front doorstep, out in the fresh air, she gives me
a consolation goodnight kiss on the cheek, with "*Mazel tov
un zei mir gezund un shtark*." Good luck and go in strength.
But, ever mindful of her position, she puts a finger to her full
wide lips, "*Zug goornisht*." Say nothing.

I'm out the door before I even realize Mary did actually give me a choice, either the bonus or herself . . . and, a conditioned reflex, I went with the more reasonable option, the money, my escape hatch to nowhere.

PART FIVE

PART FIVE

38

Cold War Sex
in a Lonelier Place

I regret to say that we of the FBI are powerless to act in cases of oral-genital intimacy, unless it has in some way obstructed interstate commerce.

—J. Edgar Hoover

Carl Benton Reid (as Capt. Lochner): You're told that the girl you were with last night was found in Benedict Canyon, murdered . . . What's your reaction? . . . A couple of feeble jokes. You puzzle me, Mister Steele.

Humphrey Bogart (as Dixon Steele): Well, I grant you, the jokes could've been better, but I don't see why the rest should worry you . . . that is, unless you plan to arrest me on lack of emotion.

—From *In a Lonely Place* (1950), directed by Nicholas Ray. Art Smith, the actor who plays Bogart's Hollywood agent, is blacklisted.

M Y CONSTANT COMPANION these days is a six-inch-long yellow-striped, bloodshot-eyed mud turtle with stinkpot anal glands still intact who found me when I almost ran over him on one of my solitary drives into the Mojave

Desert, out past Twentynine Palms and Barstow. Buddy lives
in a Sunkist orange box by the sun-facing front window of
my new digs at the Andalusia Gardens apartments, the closest I could find to Bogart's Spanish patio-garden apartment
in *In a Lonely Place*, at $150 a month for a one bedroom
with views of the Hollywood Hills and downstairs an underground garage for Ray's and my power-lift equipment, and
for good/bad karma it's just down the street from F. Scott
Fitzgerald's old pad. The Andalusia, with its tiled walkway
and sparkling stone fountain and hanging bougainvillea,
is an almost exact copy of where Bogart tries to strangle
Gloria Grahame (also a Jaffe client) in the next apartment.
When one of the movie characters says of Bogart, ". . . *he's
exciting because he isn't quite normal*," Ray Kovacs and I
always give a big yelp of recognition. We've seen it half a
dozen times; that's us up on the screen.

After rolling up my Jaffe calls I talk to my turtle Buddy
on lonely nights when I toddle home adrenalin-drained from
work, feed him grass, clover, and fresh spinach, pour out
my troubles to him, swallow my dinner of White Horse and
buttermilk, throw off my agency uniform for a T-shirt, jeans
and rubber-soled (from Goodyear Tires) huaraches, bring
out my drum sticks to play along with Dexter Gordon's
"Cherokee" on my EP Autorama player-radio, and brace
myself for a night of . . .

. . . Mutt and Jeff's predictable surprise visits or . . .

. . . the Ladies Auxiliary or . . .

. . . the Omegas minus Ray who has vanished somewhere,

. . . whichever rolls out first.

In a pervasive culture of betrayal Omega's tight little loyal group is my only artwork and deepest commitment where Ray, Sparky, Pete, Barney, Jimmy, Irwin, Joe Ferguson the French horn player, and Dorothy Healy are the only people I totally trust aside from my steady girl Terry. We have no "aims" or "goals"—just engage in minor, brainless acts of sabotaging the machine. (Like scattering leaflets from a light plane over the city just to let them know we're alive; defacing Hollywood Walk of Fame terrazzo-and-brass stars with the word "fink" on the names of informers, etc.) If there's such a thing as collective love, this is mine.

Because my phone line is tapped, on Friday nights we speak VERY LOUDLY to the apartment walls like lunatics. Before he disappeared Ray Kovacs did a persuasive Slavic accent as a Russian spy. "*Sergei, ze sheep leafs at meednight. Bring ze blooprintz.*" And then, boom!, all of us, except Dorothy who disapproves of pranks that fail to advance an agenda, scramble into Ray's Olds convertible and zoom downtown to the Sixth Street bridge where, from under a nearby viaduct, we spy on our spies, the FBI doofuses disguised as sewer repair men and street cleaners with telltale buzz cuts, we've all seen *The House on 92nd Street* and *Walk East on Beacon*, the Feds are aching to nab the suspected Soviet agents, us. What a hobby for grown men, them and us.

But other nights belong to . . .

39

The Women

THE WOMEN'S NATION AT THIS TIME

US women's wages are a little more than half of what men earn. Wives normally do not spend money without their husbands' consent or walk into a bar alone. Quilted boned bras are called brassieres, also worn are girdles, petticoats, "New Look" ankle-length high-waisted or pencil skirts and dresses pairing nicely with a belt and tucked-in shirt, classic cardigan and pedal pushers, cats-eye glasses, "hose" with garter belts, stiletto heels or ballet slippers, and cinched waists. Clitoral versus vaginal orgasm is regarded as "unwomanly" or clinically neurotic and highly upsetting to some men and most doctors. Abortions are illegal and bloody. Women with LSD, low sexual desire for men, are called "frigid" or "lesbian"; women who like sex are "nymphomaniacs"; women who for whatever reason reject a man may be called a frigid lesbian nymphomaniac. What women are told about themselves they tend to believe.

Boys have trucks . . . Girls have dolls
Boys are strong . . . Girls are graceful
Boys are doctors . . . Girls are nurses
Boys are policemen . . . Girls are meter maids
Boys are football players . . . Girls are cheerleaders
Boys are pilots . . . Girls are stewardesses
Boys are Presidents . . . Girls are First Ladies
Boys fix things . . . Girls need things fixed
Boys can eat . . . Girls can cook
Boys invent things . . . Girls use what boys invent
Boys build houses . . . Girls keep houses
—from *I'm Glad I'm a Boy! I'm Glad I'm a Girl!*
(1970), a children's book by Whitney Darrow Jr.

WITH MALICE AND irony the women in my life call themselves . . .

40

The Ladies Auxiliary

S ELF-AWARE AND (MORE or less) single, they have
lives that intersect on my bed. Knowing but not knowing about one another, they come and go according to *their*
schedules, not mine. I'm a convenient stopover on their
way to the altar of marrying some other man, marriage the
end of their brief vacation being responsible only for themselves. I'm the one acted upon; they demand no preliminar-
ies, no advance warning. No candlelight dinners, long drives
to the beach at sunset, lingering kisses, penetrating gazes.
Minimum pillow talk, just get to it. They want to be taken,
not possessed.

Why me now? I don't have movie-star looks, haven't
much money, and—as Anita, B-Jay, Kelly, Petra, Vanessa,
and the others acidly remind me—I'm not spectacularly
hung. Probably they feel safe because I'm such poor husband
material. The other factor in my favor is that, compared to
most other guys, I have nothing to lose. The Omega's Barney
Bialik, my on-call free-of-charge shrink still in psychiatric

training, calls it "poor impulse control"; Mary Baker calls it "steel balls" because in dealing with customers my lying imagination knows no limits; maybe it's my politics which I hide from the Industry but not the women.

❖

IT's ABSURD TO accuse these women of making a "political statement" with their bodies, because they are neither activists nor interested in the blacklist syndrome. Only Anita who makes her living from the film business is angrily aware ("The schmucks brought it on themselves"); for the other women, as for most Americans, the mass purges don't exist except possibly as a soon forgotten newspaper or TV item from a remote planet far away. Yet, is it possible, just a theory, that the sex we practice is a vague sort of challenge— against what?—to a prevailing culture? By wantonly going up against *Ozzie & Harriet* and *Father Knows Best* we're doing a baaaad thing. Logically we should go all the way, fisting and cross-dressing and gender reversal and whips and handcuffs, but none of us are willing or ready to go into such (as yet) unexplored territory. The most abnormal thing we do is what we do. Way way out there on the edge of the culture the Beats and their women may be doing something else, but not us.

"Do they get any pleasure?" my mother Jennie inquires when I explain some of this to her. How does a man ever know?

Agreed, there's a fevered quality to it, on a kitchen table, an office floor, a broom closet at a PTA meeting, behind drapes at a cocktail party, under the Moses sculpture at a Forest Lawn funeral, absolutely no talk of commitment or transcendental love; instead, a giving and receiving of guilt-free (we hope) ravishment, a pleasant enough defiance of the (alleged) norm. God knows the women are not revolutionaries, yet fumbling and groping, we seem to be enacting eroticism for a future time. B-Jay, Kelly, Rhoda, Anita, Petra, Van, Annie, Marcia, and Laura, their arms, breasts, hair, lips, cunts, legs wrapped around my neck: how is it that Mary Baker and Sam Jaffe fail to detect their pubic perfume that clings to me like Saran wrap, intoxicating, repugnant, life-giving?

All the women except Bobette (with the eyepatch), a numbers cruncher at Rand, and B-Jay, the chain-smoking fashion journalist, work at jobs way below their competence.

Over time, Laura, B-Jay, and Rhoda idly "confess" that they are also bisexual, a new concept to me. When Terry once suggested I might have a suspect itch for Ray, I was so horrified that I backhoed the whole issue out of mind. Bisexual means what? B-Jay says, "Relax, honeybun . . . it's only the wave of the future." Not mine!

Are there angry scenes? Sometimes. Their fury tends to explode over what they complain is my emotional detachment from the act. B-Jay nicked her wrist with a kitchen knife in a feeble suicide attempt, yelping in outrage when it actually stung. Laura, dying of leukemia, even in her disabled condition tried to run me down in her Nash Rambler on Kelly's front lawn. That sort of thing.

We are well met.

I'm like a well-recommended dentist or plumber passed hand to hand.

❖

AS WITH THE FBI, it happens like this:

Knock, knock. No warning phone call, no "Are you free tonight?" She just walks in, drops her handbag, accepts a drink or two, browses my magazine rack—*Neurotica, The Nation, Rod & Custom, Muscle Power, I.F. Stone's Weekly*—and it's on.

The other Omegas are unsympathetic to my traffic management issue. Joe the musician: "If you ask me, you're all fucked up. So are they. Like attracts like." Sparky: "It's your vibes. They like fearless guys. They don't know you like we do." Jimmy, the math whiz and conscientious objector, takes out a pencil with a sheet of blank paper and draws a graph. "See where these lines intersect? Here is 19 June 1953 when the Rosenbergs got executed at Sing Sing. Here is 1 March 1954 when the United States exploded the world's first hydrogen bomb. According to you, in this entire period of busy sexual intercourse, this intersection of X and Y represents your peak of activity which exactly corresponds to the period between the Rosenbergs and the H-bomb explosion. There's your correlation." Irwin the lawyer concludes, "Count your blessings and don't worry about fender benders."

41

The Price of Love

"FREE LOVE" COMES at a cost. Two of the Ladies Auxiliary have undergone illegal, expensive life-threatening abortions from previous lovers. That's where Barney Bialik enters their picture. Barney has a self-chosen calling, aside from his psychiatric internship, which is that he's a pregnancy terminator, a nonprofit avocation—almost a crusade. Charging only for gas money, he escorts women across the border to Tijuana, two hours' drive south, where a Mexican doctor does it. These cross-border trips are his "mission" because he saw his older sister sicken and almost die from a back-alley butcher. The thing about all this is that Barney, normally low-key and self-effacing, travels in an all-black Zorro-type costume—he even keeps a black mask in the car. I didn't say we weren't weird.

And then there's always Terry, *primus inter pares*, first among equals, a legal phrase I've learned to insert in agency contracts. What makes her so special? Two for the price of one: she was Ray's girl, now mine; she calls it homoerotic whatever that means. Terry's given to volcanic rages. With Mediterranean features, she had her Nefertiti's great nose surgically lopped off, eyebrows thinned, name Anglicized, when like so many other young Jewish women, feeling themselves ugly, and in some cases not wanting to be visibly associated with the Jewish spies the Rosenbergs, de-Judaized themselves at about the same time as some Jewish men Americanized their names. The ferocity of sex between Terry and me—no holds barred, no insult too degrading—is our most violent playing out of "boxcar love," the frantic homicidal coupling of the transported women and men whose distant fate in wartime Eastern Europe shapes our nightmares. Even now in Congress seven liberal Democrats are promoting a Detention Act to put subversives like Terry and me into internment camps in a "national emergency." Terry broods that they'll shave her head. Girls! It will grow back again, I say, and she glares at me as if I am the enemy.

42

The Crash

TERRY AND I have split up dozens of times, for every reason or none, but something always seems to drive us back together.

It happens one night. Omega member Pete and I are in his rattletrap Hudson going down Melrose Avenue after furtively slapping posters (NIX ON NIXON) on the big white Gower Street wall of Columbia Pictures, my old employer. Nothing so pleasing as revenge politics. "What the hell is that?" Pete asks as we pass a corner where a red Mercury coupe is upended on its roof. Not a soul else is around. This is Los Angeles when the carpet is rolled up at sundown.

Pete and I jump out to render aid. With dread I see that the wrecked car is Terry's familiar cherry-red Mercury coupe. Trapped, she's sprawled all over the inside of the Mercury's roof. Pete, former 11th Airborne, is built like a blocking tackle. Putting our backs into it, we rock the Mercury back and forth on its roof until with one gigantic heave we roll it over on its side, and we drag Terry out. Conscious but shocked, she refuses to be taken to a hospital.

Pete and I lay her out on the street, and he uses his flashlight to go over her bruised and shaken body. She gives him a weak smile. "Get your pervert hands off me." We transport Terry to my place at the Andalusian apartments where Pete, who has a pregnant wife in the Valley, goes home.

One look at Terry in her torn clothes makes me regret we didn't get her to a hospital. She's shivery and shaking all over, her eyes astonished at her near-death experience. Was it an accident or . . . ? We'll never know because all Terry says is that she never saw the vehicle that broadsided her into the tree and drove off without stopping. Mutt and Jeff strike again or just plain accident?

On my bed I cover her body and draw up a chair and hold her hand which is like ice. Her skin is yellow, her eyes incredibly large on me. "Take off my clothes," she whispers. "I'm so cold."

Carefully, under the blanket, I strip her naked. She throws off the cover to let me look at her shaking from top to toe. Slowly, nude, she calms.

"They tried to kill me . . . Bring me back," she urges.

I strip off and just stand there examining her damaged body with purple hematomas all over her flesh. The sight of it turns me on. She's turned on by watching me being turned on by her being damaged. They should shoot me for what I'm thinking.

I climb into bed beside her, holding her as carefully as I can.

"No. All the way on top."

"I'll hurt you."

Her eyes are burning.

I pump life into her. Don't care if it hurts. The best sex we've ever had.

The last thing she says before coming is "We deserve each other."

43

A Visit from a Constant Reader

LONELY NIGHTS AT the Andalusia Gardens—no women or Terry or the Omegas—I hammer on an ancient Corona Standard portable to hear the satisfying sound of cannon-shot keys. Just to mess with my spooks, I'll ball up the carbon copies and scrunch them in the garbage can downstairs in the back alley for the Feds to scavenge through. My readership of two—you have to start somewhere.

Then I begin all over again retyping lines from a Hemingway story in an attempt to catch his disease. "*The hills across the valley of the Ebro were long and white . . .*"

A surprise, Jeff is solo tonight. Seeing him again is a relief in a way. These Fed visits anchor me.

Clears his throat. "May I come in?"

He eases in, humorless eyes scanning, never cracks a smile. My hands, soon to grow a rash, feel a warm blood rush.

Jeff stops short at Buddy's Sunkist orange box nest by the

front window and examines my Mojave turtle as if planning to insert a radio bug in its carapace. Careful, Jeff, turtles are notorious farters, just think of the static.

"Can I touch him?" he asks.

"Sure," I say. "But he bites."

When Jeff inserts a finger under Buddy's beaked nose the turtle's jaws clamp on and won't let go; Jeff lifts Buddy and stares him in the eye and then swings his hand to toss him off. No luck, he has to use both hands to detach Buddy and place him firmly back in the moss-sided box.

Jeff inspects his finger. "Mighty strong little critter, Clancy. Hangs in there, like you."

Without asking permission he browses among the bookshelves.

"Nothing there, Jeff," I say, using my nickname for him for the first time in his hearing.

"Jeff. Like Jeffrey Hunter. Ever see him in *Princess of the Nile*?" his back still to me.

Fan-tastic, he's a movie bug, too. Following Jeff's eyes around the apartment, I wonder if there are any incriminating bras or leaflets lying around.

Jeff asks if he can remove his tie.

Oh?

He draws up a canvas chair.

❖

CLEARS HIS THROAT again. "May I ask your denomination?"

"Five, tens and twenties," I say. An old joke. With equal civility: "None of your damn business."

Should not have cursed, gives him an edge.

"I'm a Jew. Jewish. That denomination enough for you?"

"I'm Mormon," he says. "A Mormon," he corrects himself.

"Ah yes, Joe Smith, the golden plates, angel Moroni."

Jeff sets his formidable large teeth. "It's Joseph Smith." Then adds: "I'm from Abraham, Millard County, in Utah."

"I'm from Chicago, but you already know that."

"Right. Last known address"—as if reading an index card in his brain—"1404 South Kedzie." Only ten years out of date. Don't expect miracles.

He keeps twisting his head as if he missed something or is consulting with himself about whether coming here is such a good idea after all.

"You have to understand about Mormons," he begins.

All I can think of is his gun and does the Church of Latter Day Saints sanction shooting the unsaved? He'd never shoot me. Never.

He leans forward. Why is he sweating?

"Man to man?"

Without waiting for my response he blurts: "We're supposed to have marriage in our thoughts and prayers."

We? The FBI. Ah, no, LDS.

He says, "*Keep me, O Lord, from the hands of the wicked; preserve me from the violent man; who have purposed to overthrow my goings.*"

What is he talking about?

Jeff recrosses his legs and holds his knee almost like a pistol pointed at me. "Alma. Psalms 140. Alma's our prophet."

He smiles for the first time. "We don't date except within our own kind. And our teaching is, unmarried sex is impure carnality, a sin next to murder. You see the problem."

Which is?

"My partner and I noticed a procession of young women in and out of your place."

"Russian spies?" I suggest.

Jeff's sense of humor was extracted like an infected tooth at the Quantico FBI Academy.

"At first we thought you operated a house of ill repute for illegal gain. That's breaking the law. White Slave Traffic Act of 1910." Al Capone they nailed for income tax invasion, and me for taking girlfriends across a state line?

"I never," I say.

"You took Terry to visit Hoover Dam on, um . . ." he searches his file-card memory, ". . . in March this year."

My god, they think I'm trying to blow up our water supply.

A long silence. This is costing him. Almost a sigh: "Just someone in the movies."

"Excuse me?"

If a voice can perspire it's Jeff's. "Socially. With a movie actress. She doesn't have to be a star. You can set it up." He adds, "I'd appreciate it."

He's blushing. My God, he envies me.

The words are out of my mouth without thinking. "No problem."

He gets up to go, all FBI again. "I'll be in touch."

Any fool can see he wants to turn me into an FBI asset. But what if I turn him? I phone Anita, the Jaffe secretary whose dad is a Burbank policeman, good fit there.

"You high again on all those uppers?" is her first response, but she's intrigued. "Pop would love it. He's always trying to fix me up with cops." She thinks. "Well, why not? Haven't had a real date in ages. Who's paying?"

It's a possible police trap, I warn. "Fat chance," she responds. "Dad's a watch commander and Uncle Anthony is Secret Service." She thinks: "A setup? I love it!"

Terry is my date because she's already a "person of interest" with nothing to lose, and like Anita is turned on by risk.

A few evenings later Jeff in a charcoal-flannel suit comes by not in the government's familiar Chevy coupe but a Dodge Meadowlark, and in East Hollywood we pick up Anita, tall, olive-skinned, late twenties, great figure, Armenian, almost an actress, bubbling over with chat.

Right away she tells Jeff that her uncle Anthony is Secret Service.

Jeff, in his high-pitched voice, "What detail?"

Anita, dressed to kill in an off-the-shoulder peasant blouse and full dirndl skirt, in the passenger seat next to him, places her hand on the armrest behind his head and pats his buzz cut. "That's why it's called secret."

Jeff clams up. Anita caresses his neck, "That's a joke, son."

We take Jeff to a couple of jazz clubs but he's bored by Bud Shank and Gerry Mulligan—is he a Lawrence Welk fan? So we end up at the corporate man's favorite faux Polynesian hangout, Don the Beachcomber in Hollywood, mai tais (feh) and rumaki (double feh) which he keeps ordering because he loves that garbage. For the first time he relaxes in the club's coconut tree-and-hula-skirt atmosphere. Maybe he'll forget all about sex with Anita who's been sizing up his bi- and triceps and clearly is game. His only problem is the roving club photographer in a grass skirt who comes by to snap us at ten bucks a pop, Jeff looks like he's fainting when he dives under the tablecloth pretending to look for his wallet.

The next day at the office I pull aside Anita who reports, "Okay, right, he takes me home, and keeps asking if I'm in the movies, I say yes I'm an agent's secretary and deal with stars all the time, Jane Russell and Rock Hudson blah blah, but he wants to know am I up there on the screen and he won't let go, after all he's paid to interrogate people, right?, and when I say no, I just work the phones but have career hopes, his face falls, you know for a short guy he's got an awful lot of face, the thing is he wants to make it with a movie star . . ."

"Well, did you?" I ask.

She lets out a big breath. "Only because I needed the sleep. He lasts all of, what, thirty seconds, reminds me of you."

"You didn't call him a lousy lover the way you do me or say anything about Mormons, did you?"

"Not to worry, honeybun, afterwards I told him he was terrific and sent him home to hunt more little commies like you."

She's omitting something, I can tell. What really happened between them? "I can take it," I promise.

Anita says, "My experience with you is no you can't," and walks away.

Something tells me that Anita has made me an enemy for life in Jeff.

Proof: those damn headlights.

When all else fails late at night my other habit is to jump into the Pontiac to pelt down Olympic in the milky mist, Angelenos call it marine layer, to the beach, timing the lights perfectly and taking the curves fast on PCH down to Malibu and back, Dexxie daring. I'd like to pick up Ray Kovacs on the way, he and his *Tequila con Vibora* are ideal beach companions, except he hasn't been around much since his trial. I miss him so much. Alone, I'll park on a little bluff above Topanga Beach and stroll down for body surfing, nothing gnarly, just jogging under the cold dim moon along the water's edge trailing a wet bedsheet to catch the breeze and fill it with air and skid my body along the shoreline.

But ever since our double date the canary-yellow government-owned Chevy coupe, with Jeff at the wheel, has been tailing me all over LA, to the market, to Tommy the barber, the Jaffe office, I can feel Jeff's rage, blaming me for whatever happened or didn't between him and Anita. Now, on PCH, he's on my bumper and making me drive blind in the night fog.

No way can my six-cylinder 80BHP tired ol' hoss outrun their 437V8 engine, so it's nothing for Jeff to flash his brights blasting into my rearview mirror until with zero visibility I have to shield my eyes with my stick shift hand while the Chevy stubbornly tailgates. I'm tempted to brake hard and bill their insurance company for the damage, but who knows if the Feds carry liability?

When I fake them by twisting the wheel off onto a narrow layby at Las Flores Canyon, they tip my right rear bumper and nudge me back onto the highway until I'm in the oncoming lane and about to collide head-on with a Mack big rig. Yow! I tug and heave the wheel to get back in my lane a split second before a smashup.

These guys are trying to kill me.

❖

THEY'RE NOT THE only ones trying. Another above-ground atom bomb test at the Nevada Proving Ground lights up the eastern sky over the Hollywood mountains. White stucco apartment walls around the Andalusia Gardens explode fluorescent. We live in fear and denial. Odd how nobody at Jaffe ever talks about the "nuclear danger." Am I the only one who reads a newspaper? But we have more important things on our minds, like how to find work for Barbara Stanwyck, will the blacklist gods confuse our boss Sam Jaffe with the blacklisted actor Sam Jaffe, will client Joe Cotton be tainted by association with Orson Welles, how can we keep client Gloria Grahame from more face-surgery and Bogie from grabbing any old job for the money, what are we going to do with Ginger Rogers, why doesn't the audience see Ray Danton as a potential superstar . . . ?

PART SIX

44

The Storm Subsides, Sunrise over Malibu

Even the darkest night will end and the sun will rise.

—Victor Hugo, *Les Misérables*

T HE GRAY KILLER smaze is clearing. Hard to absorb at first because a better time creeps up on you unawares. For Sunday runners like Ray and me "the new day dawning" begins, improbably, when a gawky English medical student named Roger Bannister scales the Everest of milers by shattering the four-minute record with an impossible, exhilarating 3.59.4. Then the Nazi SS's favorite American, Senator Joe McCarthy, flames out on nationwide TV in the Army-McCarthy hearings after lawyer Joe Welch demolishes him (*"Senator, you've done enough. Have you no sense of decency, sir? At long last, have you left no sense of decency?*); followed by the Supreme Court decision in *Brown vs. Board of Education*. And the next year Rosa Parks refuses to go to the back of a Montgomery, Alabama, bus, and a court

orders Herman Kutcher, a legless combat GI and Socialist
Workers Party member fired by the VA for "disloyalty," to
get his job back. . . .

. . . And maybe a tide is turning. Even the bad Los
Angeles air feels fresher. Omega, born in battle, and until
this moment shunned by the risk-averse, almost overnight
slips from the control of us Original Gangsters to admit new
recruits made braver by the turning tide. At first shyly, in
twos and threes, total strangers invite themselves to what
had been an exclusive elite of losers. The newcomers are
an eclectic assortment, including, God bless him, in civilian
clothes a serving US Coast Artillery colonel, and they also
include "Frank," a Communist assigned by the Party to spy
on us, which means that whoever is an undercover government agent in our group also has the duty of spying on whoever is reporting to the Party which is heavily infiltrated by
the FBI, a Krazy Kat web of deceit.

This new expanded Omega means that fresh members
feel awkward with the Omega's prevailing anarchy. Hence
they impose a Roberts Rules of Order structure, chairman,
treasurer, etc. Where's the fun in that? And what a surprise!
a USC student majoring in Business Admin volunteers as
recording secretary. Taking down all our names.

A word about plants, not the green species. Who in their
right mind would want to do this unpaid donkeywork? The
local prodigy is Mabel Leach, the county's Party member-
ship secretary who has supplied the FBI with 327 names of
LA members plus detailed biographies written by the victims
themselves. Way to go, Mabel!

Among the new group is "Dr. Mark," progressive ther-
apist-to-the-stars, who is looking at Terry and, damn her
soul, she is looking back at him.

45

Enter Doctor Charisma

M Y CAREER IS definitely on an upswing. The Christmas bonus, an agent's Holy Grail, is a thousand times more than I made as a dockside banana fiend, even more than Zack Silver's, though we don't know why since he brings in more business (Zack: "You have visibility, I just close deals"). And my Mephistopheles, Universal's Bill Alland, keeps pressing me to come work for him; while Mary and Sam hint that one day, in a distant future, if I keep my nose clean and go to more openings I could even be trusted to cover the Almightys, Metro and Fox. Sky's the limit. Agents morph into producers, producers rise to studio heads, I could own Hollywood! Louis Mayer, Harry Cohn, Jack Warner—watch out!

But my nights are desolate since Ray vanished from my life, our barbells packed in storage, while the Omega cell—a victim of its success—is splintering because new, more serious members don't share, or agree with, the original madness. And now my emotional anchor Terry Allison has abandoned me to go off with Dr. Mark.

The familiar knock! Knock!

"Clancy?"

Not Jeff this time.

"Yeah."

"Are you otherwise occupied? May I come in?"

"I'm dead. Try Forest Lawn."

It's Dr. Mark, the therapist who stole my girl.

"Can we have a mature conversation? I'd like that very much," he says.

I unhook the screen door.

He steps in to extend his hand like a car salesman. "I'm Terry's lover and her analyst."

Straightforward. Honest. The prick.

He's gorgeous, almost as good-looking as Ray except Semitic, a big head of bushy prematurely white hair, a strong-nosed face out of early Roman sculpture maybe Grecian, professionally piercing eyes, labile mouth, the full equipment.

What kind of world is it where a movie-star handsome shrink walks into your home and says I'm screwing your best girlfriend?

That hair, angel's penumbra, lean body, a beige turtle-neck sweater drapes over his shoulders like a tennis pro, pressed slacks, fashion conscious. Is Terry crazy, leaving me for this male model?

He clears his throat, introduces himself, as if he's not famous and knows it.

"My name is Maynard Goldman. I've seen you at meetings. They call me Doctor Mark. I have a practice in the medical building on Wilshire. You may have heard of it. The Primordial Tension Center? We bypass Freud and Jung and go straight down to it."

Maynard?

"I'll call you Mike," I say.

He gives a little confidential laugh that implies "the world is my patient, you among them."

Me, thinking: Why am I even talking to this *fonfer*?

Where does he get all this self-approval? To his patients, I'm told, he's Doctor Charisma, bending a wise ear to the troubles of Hollywood names like John Garfield, Sterling Hayden, even some of the Hollywood Ten, movie people under pressure. Terry being with this guy is my fault, I never got down to her primordial tension. God knows we tried.

He says, "I'm here to clear the air a little. Neither Tova nor I want any misunderstanding as a result of your long relationship with her."

Tova? Back to her roots.

I say, "You're fucking a patient and want my permission?"

He seems relaxed, long-suffering, tolerant, an easy friend and mentor with small clear infinitely understanding eyes. He forgives me but for what?

"We should attempt," he repeats, "to resolve any outstanding problem. It's part of Tova's therapy and frankly my peace of mind."

"No problem. You're fucking my girlfriend."

He is cucumber calm. "We are working through her issues in therapy. Nothing out of the ordinary. Infantile dependency, Oedipal conflict, that sort of thing." Isn't he breaking some sort of shrink law by telling me this? His unruffled manner ruffles mine.

Calmly, professorially, Bergman: "I can see why she left you."

That's it. Boils over.

"WHAT KIND OF AMERICA IS THIS? YOU COME INTO MY HOUSE AND TALK LIKE THIS TO ME AND EXPECT TO WALK OUT ALIVE?!"

His fixed smile through it all. There's something so giving, soft and supine and self-assured about this guy: Again I hallucinate: Maynard Goldman is the wave of the future. Nothing there. If I shoot him, he'll simply crumple to the floor muttering, "I accept your apology . . ."

Then it hits me. John Garfield, Sterling Hayden, Lee Cobb . . . all HUAC subpoenas and all Dr. Mark's patients.

I ask, "Are you the same shrinker who advises his patients to go to the FBI?"

His smile wavers a trifle. "I would never advise a patient against her conscience."

Uh oh.

"If Terry is called to testify, what will she do?" I ask.

"Tova will stay in therapy, with me or someone like me. It's up to her."

"No, I mean will she or won't she?"

"I'm not at liberty to discuss my patients' prognoses." But he does when he feels like it.

"Then why did you come up here?"

"As I said, to help resolve . . ."

". . . certain outstanding issues . . ."

He sighs, deeply.

At the screen door Maynard pauses. "Tova and I want only the best for you."

On the Andalusia's balcony in the darkness I measure the distance down to the cement driveway. Twenty feet, depends if he's pushed or falls. Ray—the old Ray—would kick him off and pray for a fractured skull. He'd know how to handle this *mazik*.

I call after Maynard, "Hey Mike, I hope she gives you gonorrhea the way she does everyone else!"

Halfway down he pauses to turn around.

"You're a very sick person, Sigal. Did you know that?"

Diagnosis: correct.

❖

TIRED OF PRETENDING to be cool with customers like Dr. Mark and the FBI guys, I run back into the apartment and reach deep in the closet for Zack's wife's .38, load it from a box of cartridges also hidden under the sweaters, chamber one, and get downstairs to find Goldman as he climbs into his Packard Caribbean soft top. When I stick the piece in his ear, he just turns to face me calmly. "This isn't good for her, you know," and shifts a glance over at the passenger seat where Terry stares at me. I know the look. Respect. I lower the .38.

❖

"WHAT ARE THOSE?" asks Terry a week later after she leaves Dr. Mark for me again. It was the gun that did it. Terry admires guys she fears.

These blotches? I say they're tiny microphones implanted in my body by the FBI.

She gives me a weird look.

❖

MY REFLEXES ARE geared to repression so it's not easy to adjust to a new wind of change. Paranoia has become second nature and almost a comfort

Meanwhile, there's a living to earn.

At the office the main women in my life are my clients. Maybe it's because I work for a woman (although she's hardly a feminist and would never make a special case for a woman client). Or maybe it's because Decla Dunning, Gabrielle Upton, Harriet Frank Jr., Peggy Fitts, and Mary Loos remind me of Jennie, who was out of work so long when I was growing up. These women writers would prefer a more prestigious agent like Jonny who can get them into Metro or Fox, or Zack at Columbia and Paramount, but like the Ladies Auxiliary they consider me acceptable until something better comes along.

46

She's Only a Poor Workin' Girl

Don't be frightened of me. It isn't love.

—Dorothy McGuire as sex-starved war widow Pat Luscombe
in *Till the End of Time* (1946). Actors Selena Royle and Ruth
Nelson will be blacklisted. Director Edward Dmytryk goes to
jail as one of the Hollywood Ten and then, to get back into
the industry, names twenty-six names.

M ARY BAKER IS getting tired of my lapses at client
conferences when I compulsively refer to actors by
the roles I most remember instead of by their real or stage
names, a symptom of incurable obsessive star-astigmatism. Thus, Vincent Price is "Shelby," his gigolo character
in *Laura*; Paul Henreid is "Victor" from *Casablanca*; Joe
Cotton is "Holly" from *The Third Man*; and so forth. Mary
says such slips make me sound like a "civilian," as she calls
them.

Latest incident: Mary calls me in to cool off the unhappy
actress Dorothy McGuire who is fed up playing nice girls.

No more *Claudia* and *The Enchanted Cottage*, which is how we make our money.

McGuire played a sexy, promiscuous war widow in *Till the End of Time,* but the studio bosses are so uncomfortable with their nice virgin as a whore that they've made her Waspy-clean again in *Gentleman's Agreement* and *Three Coins in the Fountain*, causing the frustrated actress to listen too closely to the siren calls of rival agencies promising they'll get her grittier, more Academy Award–winning jobs.

The first movie I saw after the army, in a thirty-six cent flea pit called Hamtramck in Detroit, was *Till the End of Time*, a B-budget weepie, about lonely McGuire's relationship with returned GI Guy Madison. Surfer-handsome Guy falls for emotionally troubled Pat Luscombe to the tune of Chopin's *Polonaise* remastered as a pop song of the film's title. (*"Till the end of time, long as stars are in the blue/Long as there's a spring of birds to sing, I'll go on loving you . . ."*) I loved the movie, loved the army, identified with the actors, and fell instantly for McGuire on screen.

With her broad forehead, pug nose, and discreet chest, she's not conventionally pretty, but walking-wounded women are my weakness. What I carried away from that cheap Hamtramck theater was an erotically charged memory of gamine-faced McGuire, stunned by grief, lying on a couch gazing up at vulnerable young Guy Madison (i.e., me), the ex GI. Un-for-get-table.

Now I've got a lunch date with heart-stopping bad-good girl Pat Luscombe to douse her restless flame.

Having again borrowed Mary's red Cadillac Coupe de Ville convertible, I'm at Scandia's smorgasbord table forty-five minutes before my reservation time, munching nervously on a *prinskorv* appetizer, knowing it's bad manners before the guest arrives. McGuire is married, but my fantasy is that if things work out, the moon in the third quadrant, I'll fuck her brains out in a rented cottage at the Garden of Allah down the Strip. My old problem, I'm in my own movie; it's so easy to slip onto the soundstage of my mind where I can control the camera, lighting, makeup.

Punctually, she arrives in a gray worsted suit with mirror buttons (have to get rid of those for a start), knee-length skirt, and ballet slippers. The outfit subdues her slim figure, but I think I can fix that.

McGuire—that is, Pat Luscombe—apologizes for being on time, "a character flaw my husband is always telling me," what is she afraid of with this husband stuff? as she puts out a small ungloved hand for me to accept. Ah, Pat the born schoolmarm, a subtle reprimand to me for having started without her.

We're in a snug booth away from foot traffic. She's even more attractive in life than in the movies. Something appealingly neurotic in those large attentive, come-to-me-but-not-too-close eyes. Hot damn!

After our first course Pat Luscombe puts down her fork. "I've been rattling on about me and you haven't even said a word, Mr. Sigal. Cat's got your tongue?"

Gawping again.

Snapping out of it, I go into an agent's practiced stay-with-us-and-we'll-take-care-of-you sales patter. Pat unbuttons her jacket; she's wearing a white silk blouse open at the throat, I can't stand it. Small breasted, but this one has brains.

She's getting edgy. We've been drinking *Schnapps*, perhaps too many for an afternoon. Her round Irish face is flushed; I'm sweating bullets under my wool suit.

Finally: We stop talking.

"Yes, ma'am?" Why do I address her like my mother or a schoolteacher?

She puts both delicate hands on the white clothed table.

"Were you in the service, Mr. Sigal?"

"Yes'm."

"I thought so." Long pause. "You know," very slowly, softly, almost a whisper, "I am not Pat Luscombe. Only soldiers think so. Dear heart—" She called me dear! "—I am an actress. My job is to impersonate people who are not me." She puts on a trace of Brooklyn accent. "Jus' a poor woikin' goil."

Dorothy McGuire reaches across the table and takes my hand. Her throaty, thin, actress voice—I can see how she uses it to trap men—is warm and sincere.

"I am so sorry I am who I am."

She pats my hand maternally, rises, leans over, kisses my cheek and heads for the exit with some excuse she's late for an appointment. Bet she is. Sorry, that is.

In the end, Dorothy, who isn't Pat, stays with the Jaffe office and, accepting her career karma, submits to our casting her with Gary Cooper as a Quaker wife in *Friendly Persuasion*; she suffers so well.

That same week, on my own time, I track her down in *Gentleman's Agreement* at a Beverly Boulevard revival house. McGuire, here called Kathy Lacey, as usual super-Protestant, falls for equally gentile Gregory Peck, who is a journalist pretending to be Jewish for an exposé story. In the movie McGuire can't handle Peck's "Jewishness" because in her experience Jews are loud, vulgar, smelly, and unpredictable while Kathy likes her life polite, orderly, inoffensive. Or as Peck-the-fake-Jew points out, *"The Kathys everywhere are afraid of getting the gate . . . from their little groups of nice people."*

Of course. Right. Dorothy-Pat-Kathy is an anti-Semite. She doesn't like pushy Jews.

So that explains it.

47

Baby Face

Yeah, I'm a tramp. . . . Ever since I was fourteen, what's it been? Nothing but men! Dirty rotten men! And you're lower than any of them. I'll hate you as long as I live!

—Barbara Stanwyck in *Baby Face* (1933), story by Darryl Zanuck, who as head of 20th Century Fox went along with the blacklist but privately helped some victims

URSULA GIBBONS, GLAMOUR girl of my writer clients, is blonde, busty, baby faced, blue-eyed, vital and oh, by the way, competent. I've got her because no other agent is able to raise her above $250 a week, which in Hollywood is a starvation wage. In prehistory half the Hollywood screenwriters were women—Frances Marion, Anita Loos, Jeanie MacPherson were Triple-A list—but my current client list is almost entirely men.

When I take Ursula around to producers' offices, the problem is immediately obvious.

"They want to screw but not hire me," Ursula complains with some justice.

Who can blame them? She shows up for meetings in above-the-knee tight skirts and form-hugging blouses that emphasize her fine chest, and has a way of cocking her head at men that seems come-hither but actually is a slight myopia. When I warn her about this she says, "That's just you. Sex on your mind all the time."

She needs a paying assignment because she has a disabled husband at home, and double-tithes the Catholic church where she is a devout congregant. So at the same time that she resents having to put herself out there sexually, she'll tease, flirt, laugh at dirty jokes, and even wear fishnet stockings to story conferences.

Her rationale is: "Look, do you know how hard it is for a woman to work in this town? Once I get them staring down my cleavage at least they look at me. If they want to sleep with me, that's fine, they never will. I'm faithful to my faithless husband. Jesus has His cross to bear, Greg is mine. That's where you as my agent come in. I show them a bit of leg, you pitch my talent, and we pray the dice roll in my favor. Jews pray, don't they?"

What if a producer hires her expecting sex?

She says, "Father O'Neill at Good Shepherd, his eyes undress me, too, in the confessional, you should hear the things he asks me. Men since puberty have been doing it to me. I'm not going to hide my charms behind 'lady writer' oo la la. But once I cocktease a producer into hiring me, he's got a right to expect real hard work from me, okay?"

❖

ON PASSOVER THE Jaffe office is eerily empty. Out of respect the few non-Jewish agents and secretaries are out today. Alone, I snoop through other agents' "To Do" calendars; I'm pretty sure they spy on mine, too. It's holiday quiet, and I'm so absorbed I don't hear Mary Baker also going through their Wheeldexes. We see each other at the same time; neither makes a move to the other. Then, as in a really bad movie, the earth shakes, shivers, and sways. Earthquake. A what? 4.9. The Jaffe building goes up and down like a ship in a squall, Mary and I stagger slightly and stare at each other through the waves of motion. The quake subsides, the structure seems to heave a sigh and comes to rest again. I'm on an earthquake high. Surely Mary must feel me floating over to her on an erotic charge despite what happened at her house? She walks toward me to get to her office, pauses, this is it, I'm in a fever of excitement, she says, "Ah Preilichen Pesach, kid. Next time stay home for the High Holidays. Otherwise it looks bad to the clients," and shuts the door behind her.

Kid, once more.

❖

POOR MARY BAKER. I'm still making my craving for her so crudely obvious that she is compelled to get me out of the office . . . and out of her hair.

48

The Man Killer from Double Indemnity

Fred MacMurray (as Walter Neff): You'll be here too?

Barbara Stanwyck (as Phyllis Dietrichson): I guess so, I usually am.

MacMurray: Same chair, same perfume, same anklet?

Stanwyck: I wonder if you know what I mean.

MacMurray: I wonder if you wonder.

—From *Double Indemnity* (1944); Co-star Edward G. Robinson was forced to clear himself by naming Communist sympathizers

M Y BOSS SAM Jaffe in his time has with his fists courageously fought off the armed gangsters who infested the early movie industry. But these days he turns to quivering Jell-o on hearing the soft metallic clickety-click of footsteps descending on the internal circular staircase from the poop deck where the TV department is located and where his TV agents go hungry for want of raw meat. Sam's ear is tuned to the warning sound of the iron stairs because they signal that his restless television soldiers are rattling down with yet another scheme for pushing us into the future and away from the agency's comfort zone of old-style feature films.

Sam (and I) despise TV. He calls television *ayin hara*, the Evil Eye, tube-eyed assassin of his traditional way of life and business style, he won't have one in his Bel-Air mansion and I threw out my $15 used b&w w/rabbit ears when Kukla, Fran & Ollie's singing Christmas carols out of season drove me nearly insane. Mr. Jaffe doesn't hate money, it's just that he is a product, and master, of the long-established hierarchical studio system with movie stars as immutable as the cosmos itself, or so it seems until the Evil Eye takes over.

What is Sam's—and my—world coming to?

In their hearts the Jaffe partners know TV production is moving from New York to LA, and Hollywood stars are thinking the unthinkable as their feature roles dry up: "Get me television!"

First and foremost, our Barbara Stanwyck, once Hollywood's highest paid actress, now forty-four, an ex-wife divorced by a former husband for a younger woman and herself into an affair with an actor half her age (Robert Wagner, they met recently on shooting *Titanic*), and she has nothing to do but drink and *hock* Sam ten times a day for a job, any job, something, for God's sake, Sam, anything.

Intensely loyal and feeling her despair, Sam for the first time, very reluctantly, gives the thumbs-up to his two TV agents to dream up a half-assed TV western series for Barbara to keep her in work. It only requires an in-house Jaffe-appointed "associate producer" to protect the agency's interests. At our Tuesday staff meeting Sam pleads for a volunteer while we all examine our fingernails because no self-respecting agent will take a pay cut for a job designed for idiots.

Silence in the room. Mary's gaze fastens on me, which Sam follows with his eyes. The platoon relaxes.

I'm drafted.

"Aw, Sam . . ."

Sam points his finger at me. "No arguments. You owe me." He's right.

Afterwards, in Sam's office I joke that at least I'll get to meet Stanwyck. Sam says, "Over my dead body!"

That's because Stanwyck was married to the ultra-conservative actor Robert Taylor, who betrayed fellow actors to the House Committee, and she herself has just wrapped a B-minus picture with her personal friend Ronnie Reagan. Both Stanwyck and Robert Taylor are staunch members of the fang-dripping Motion Picture Alliance for the Preservation of American Ideals, founded and funded by Walt Disney, John Wayne, and the actor Ward Bond who has appointed himself High Judge and Executioner of industry leftists; if they're lucky, Bond "clears" them, or best of all lets them appear in one of his films which saves their career. His horse-riding "Hollywood Hussars" spend their weekends practicing cavalry charges to repel a Red Army invasion . . . of Encino.

TALK ABOUT THE lion's den.

My instructions as Stanwyck's associate producer, a nonsense title paying less money, are to dig up story material where Barbara looks commanding on a horse and still sexy in a ten-gallon hat, and to cast her on the Joan Crawford principle with a non-dominant male actor, Stuart Whitman, but above all, I must keep away from her like she's Typhoid Mary. You never know who leaks files to whom.

My new office is a dusty cubbyhole in a small rented mid-city studio where the series is already in preproduction and where tired and harried pulp magazine editors trudge in and out lugging suitcases bulging with tear-sheets from Louis L'Amour, *Ladies Home Journal*, and the *Saturday Evening Post*, anything western and womanish. "This month," they'll pitch me, "I got two rodeo queens, a traveling lady preacher, a dance hall girl with a crippled child, a sheriff's widow who hunts down his killers . . . two for five hundred bucks whaddaya got to lose?" The way commissions are split the original writer is lucky to get $50 or $100.

The on-set line producer, in charge of logistics, is Jack Denove, a tough, experienced TV guy who on my very first day busts into my tiny lair, locks the door behind him, and sticks his fist in my face: "You ignorant shitface, I know all about you! You know nothing about television production! Just stay out of my way, hear? Or I'll crush you!" And storms out. My face burns with the truth of Denove's insult, my first Hollywood experience of being found out because up to now no one has had the guts to call my bluff since theirs might be called. Should I run after Denove and hit him to avenge my honor? He may be shorter than me but has the solid heft of a Mickey Cohen.

Jennie speaks into my ear: "Swallow it. *Do what you have to do to make it happen.*"

Screw Denove, what does he know except a thousand times more about TV? But, dammit, I am an associate producer, a title to live up to, it's who I am for now, licensed to creep around banks of equipment to watch the strong, sexual, alluring Stanwyck—in real life a rather small gray-haired lady now in fringed chamois skirt and cowgirl boots who moves effortlessly on her chalk lines, handles herself modestly, businesslike, no prima donna, just one of the crew, pausing between setups to ask advice of the key grip for how best to light herself, a collaborator, a mensch not a Star.

Where is my Raphaelita, the dashing senorita from *Message to Garcia* who in ripped silk shirt, jodhpurs, and boots first raised my little flag? And sassy Sugarpuss O'Shea in *Ball of Fire*, seductive fraudster in *The Lady Eve*? Never mind. She's speaking lines I bought for her, I, moi, me, associate producer.

She may be a fall-down drunk at home but not here in the Melrose Studio's cramped western stage—by rearranging walls it's a cowboy saloon or sheriff's jail or ranch house—a comedown from the vast Paramount and Metro soundstages of her past fame. Promptly and precisely she hits her chalk marks and in the enforced silence of a red-light shoot uses that wonderful snarly voice ("*Walter, we're both rotten*") so tuned into the overhanging mike boom she's inaudible from even inches away. On my hands and knees, spying, sneaking a look, I'm all star-love; she's like a great classical diva, disciplined, giving the lines no more no less than they deserve, she's a working actress. It's obvious from between-takes that the crew adores her because she is so respectful of them.

Like a secret agent, unseen, observant, I crouch amidst moveable walls and tangled power cables and dolly tracks, edging ever closer until I'm only an arm's length away.

That's when it all comes crashing down.

Her slight, querulous voice: "YOU! You there! I MEAN YOU!"

Nasal, harsh, assertive.

Stanwyck, in full western costume, catches me on my hands and knees cowering behind a wardrobe trunk. She stares down, Mae Doyle bruised by the world in *Clash by Night*.

Removing her Stetson and wig to reveal short gray hair, she looms over me, hands on hips. "You give me the horrors. Who are you and why are you hanging around? You're from *Confidential*?" The tabloid scandal magazine that ridicules older stars and in-closet gays.

I cough, blush, and get up. "No, ma'am." "Stories," I mumble. "I buy you stories."

"Speak up, man!"

"I'm your associate producer." Has there ever been a stupider line?

"Say what? Somebody's son-in-law? On my show!?"

Her frosty tone is exactly how she used her line in *The Lady Eve*, "*I need you like the axe needs the turkey.*"

I can hear the thundering herd of the Hollywood Hussars trampling my bloody corpse into the dust.

"Miss Stanwyck," I bleat, "I know all your pictures—*Double Indemnity, The Strange Love of Martha Ivers . . .*"

Bad association. In her movies, if she isn't murdering a man, she forces him to shoot her in the heart, almost a trademark. What strange, sado-masochistic impulses drive this woman?

Her sarcastic *Lady Eve* voice drips cobra venom. "A fan. How sweet."

She remembers her regal position in the industry.

Same line, but gentler. "A fan. How sweet."

I'm in love.

In a rush of words I explain my position on her show, but she imperiously cuts me off.

"These stories you buy! Drecksville." She maneuvers me against a stage wall, almost pressing her body against mine, the way Jack Warner did. I'm fainting.

"Now you listen to me. Associate producer my foot! Get this. I'm alone in a car on a dark road. I'm a doctor because we see my medical bag on the seat. My headlights pick out a body in the road. I stop, grab my bag, and run to render assistance. He's a young Marine. In uniform. Alive but hurt bad. I go back to the car and speed away, abandoning him in the road. Find me a story that tells the audience why."

"But Miss Stanwyck," I protest, "that's not a western."

She fires back, "Alright, in Texas. I'm the only doctor in town. Driving a one-horse buggy. This young cowboy lying on the trail. Wounded. I whip my horse on without stopping. All right, Mister Associate Producer or whatever you call yourself . . . why don't I stop for him?"

I don't know.

She grins triumphantly. "Ha!" is all she says and turns
on her heel.

After her retreating figure I call out, "Miss Stanwyck, do
you know why?"

She's gone.

On the following Monday I give in my notice to Sam and
Mary and go back to agenting. They're not surprised.

Sam says, "What she do, pull that old 'body in the road'
stunt?"

Mary says, "Should have warned you. We keep sending
her our best writers but they all strike out, too. Remember,
she had no schooling as a kid so she gets off twisting the
balls on our $2,000-a-week Harvard men."

Sam reaches over to rub my corporate-short hair:
"*Yiddische kopf*, you lasted longer than we expected. Come
back home and make yourself some money. Barbara will
survive."

Mary adds a note of economic reality. "But will we?"

❖

P.S.: UNLIKE BARBARA Stanwyck, who fends off lesbian
rumors by advertising her "Christian values," Mary Baker
doesn't condescend to office whispers that she may, or may
not, bat for the other team. She appears to be married to
an invisible husband, has borne children, and dresses with
a trace of Hattie Carnegie mannishness, but as Sam is fond
of saying, you see nothing, you know nothing, therefore it
doesn't exist.

49

Blazing Saddles

Cleavon Little (as new black sheriff Bart): Mornin',
ma'am. And isn't it a lovely mornin'?

Elderly Woman: Up yours, nigger.

—From Mel Brooks's *Blazing Saddles* (1974)

O F JAFFE'S 200 or more clients, not one is black
or Latino or openly homosexual. No Paul Robeson,
Rex Ingram, James Edwards or Juano Hernandez; no
Rita Moreno or Anthony Quinn; no Dietrich, Laughton,
Mercedes McCambridge, Agnes Moorehead, or Monty Clift.
The agency is no more racist than your next-door neighbor,
but business is business. Charlie Chan is still played by a
Swede, Mr. Moto by a Viennese, Cochise by a cross-dressing
Brooklyn Jew. Like the blacklist, our racial and sexual prej-
udices are subtle and assured, signaled by winks and nudges
and knowing smiles more than anything outspoken.

Except for one or two closet Republicans like Jonathan
Buck, we fourteen agents are mostly vaguely liberal

Democrats for whom prejudice does not exist if only because nonwhites do not exist in our lives except as personal maids (Mary Baker employs a full "colored" domestic staff) or as movie mammies ("Lawdy, lawdy, massuhs back fum de wars, praise Gawd!"). Although we represent white grandmotherly Jane Darwell, Mrs. Dolly in *Gone With the Wind*, the office has shown no interest in black Academy Award–winning Hattie McDaniel, black Butterfly McQueen, black Eddie "Rochester" Anderson, or black Everett Brown, who plays Big Sam the slave who saves Scarlett from rape. We'd probably make an exception for Dorothy Dandridge, but she belongs, in all senses, to director Otto Preminger, whose brother Ingo, alas, is a rival agent.

There are no black writers or directors on my personal client list; and we accidentally on purpose missed the boat on Hollywood's only black screenwriter, Carlton Moss. The single black presence in the Jaffe office is our janitor "Washington," no one bothers to ask his real name nor does he give it, who has an arrangement with Jonny Buck to shine his English-imported John Lobb shoes that Jonny leaves in the office overnight.

Hispanics, forget it, they exist a mere notch above blacks as serape-wrapped banditos in Republic serials (*"Ay, chiwahwah!"*); or at best as The Cisco Kid who at least brings humor and sex to the role; actual brown-skins live on the far side of the moon in Boyle Heights or in Tijuana where they groom studio moguls' horses at Agua Caliente racetrack. Only Ricardo Gonzales Pedro Montalbán y Merino, MGM's Mexican-born romantic lead, gets a free pass at the best Bel Air tennis clubs, and then there's always Carmen Miranda and Desi Arnaz, honorific whites. That's it.

Homos, on the other hand, are on the other hand.

Lesbians are an old Hollywood story, tolerated because they're "only" women, so who cares? Our client Judith Anderson (Mrs. Danvers in *Rebecca*), so what?, she ain't talking nor is any other Hollywood homo unless she or he desires a visit from the fiercely homo-hating LAPD. Salka Viertel, Greta Garbo's scriptwriter and lover, maintains a regular Sewing Circle in her Pacific Palisades home of like-minded women where Marlene Dietrich, Katharine Hepburn, Mary Baker (surprised to see me and claiming to look for clients), and the film director Dorothy Arzner drop in. Salka's son Tom Viertel is an old pal who has snuck me in the back door to find the place bursting with female energy and laughter.

Men count for more than women in the homo-hunt when at Jaffe staff meetings even a whisper of you-know-what can kill an actor's career; it's coded in our body language. If a certain actor or director comes up for a job, Ace Kantor makes a discreet mincing gesture, Jonny lifts an eyebrow, Phil snorts; only Zack Silver mutters, "Who cares?" and someone is sure to respond, "We need the trouble?" The rule of thumb is, as long as a homo doesn't make a tabloid nuisance of himself by getting busted in a public toilet, we ignore the existence of this widespread, underground movie-making subculture. Let's say one of our directors is up for a job with a leading he-man actor and our director is of questionable sexuality, somebody in the office will almost imperceptibly flap his arms that he's a *feigelah* (little bird) meaning a friend of Dorothy or just plain ass-fucker so we move on to a client with more hair on his chest, which of course proves nothing since at least two or three of our hunky clients secretly swing the other way.

In all this there's nothing personal or malicious, just the way it is.

Confidential tabloid magazine, whose chief writer is ex-Communist Howard Rushmore, has drawn a huge national readership mainly by shining a libelous light on nellies of both sexes and miscellaneous interracial liaisons. But nobody respectable reads *Confidential*—only everyone in America—so Vincente Minnelli, Cary and Randy, Tab and Rock, Cesar and Monty, and Marlon and Jimmy can rest easy until editor Howard Rushmore's liver gives out or someone has the balls to sue.

Screenwriters? They can bugger each other at high noon on the corner of Sunset and Vine and draw nothing but yawns, because like Hollywood women they're a subspecies. Same goes for below-the-line studio personnel like the team of talented composers, arrangers, lyricists, and dancers over at MGM known as (Arthur) "Freed's Fairies"; musical comedies would cease to exist if queers didn't make them.

My personal attitude is learned from a mother who raised me and by Chicago's hyper-macho immigrant street culture. Jennie went crazy the day she walked in to find me playing with female cutouts from the Sunday newspaper and hinging dresses on them. "Are you out of your mind?! Boys don't play with dolls!" Message received. In the army the guys caught me reading a book and listening to Toscanini at the service club and they waited until lights out to pour lighter fluid on my poncho-covered sleeping form and set me on fire. Message doubly received: violence awaits a man coloring outside the lines.

Now, this hot summer day Mary Baker asks me to hand-deliver a property, *Laurette*, a biography of the great stage actress Laurette Taylor, to the director George Cukor because the agency is anxious for a package deal with Warners who, at any given moment, want Cukor and Vivien Leigh and in the next unembarrassed breath June Allyson and one of their hack directors.

Cukor's address on Cordell Drive off Sunset is an easy stroll from the office but who walks in LA's mid-day sun? So I drive to Sunset Plaza, take a right on Doheny, park on the sloping tree-lined street. Cukor's estate is hidden behind a tall ivy wall where I walk through an unlatched gate and into a fantastic, stepped, lush Lost Horizon–type garden practically raining with azaleas, fuschsias, jingle bells, night-blooming jasmine, unnameable exotica, and an orange grove smack in the middle of the downward slope walkway. I straighten my tie, nervously rub to an impossible shine my calfskin shoes, and clear my throat of nervous phlegm because Cukor is one of the gods. I grew up on his pictures.

A big wooden door swings open and I'm confronted by a Jaffe client, angle-jawed Guy Haines, the tennis player in *Strangers on a Train* (1951), a.k.a. Farley Granger, actually wearing tennis shorts and a maroon-and-white-striped tennis sweater draped over his shoulders.

"Is Mister Cukor in?"

"Everybody's in, friend," says Guy or Farley, my star-astigmatism kicking in. I've never before met Granger, who is as beautiful in life as on film and cheerfully waves me through the foyer, past a winding staircase that surely must have been stolen from Tara in *Gone With the Wind*, which Cukor started to helm but was then fired by homophobic Clark Gable who demanded a "man's man."

Maniacally blurting, because it's how my movie-dialogue brain works, I call after Granger/Haines, "*You crazy maniac. Would you please get out of here and leave me alone!*" He turns with a puzzled half smile, his stock in trade.

I quote again, "*I have the perfect weapon right here: these two hands,*" which is what Bruno Anthony tells Guy Haines, conspiring to kill each other's woman. It always surprises me that actors don't remember key lines from their iconic pictures; Bogart couldn't either. Granger looks at me peculiarly and disappears through a Spanish archway.

On the tiled patio a poolside party is in full swing, and I recognize the white hair, ski-slope nose, and sensual lower lip to cautiously approach George Cukor, his legs crossed in his ironwork patio chair. A celebrity scene: two dozen movie people—stars! Joanna and Vincent and Greta and Marlene and Angela and Agnes and Ross—and everybody looks so confident as if they belong. I push the *Laurette* biography onto Cukor's lap. "From Mary Baker, sir," I stutter like the Western Union telegraph boy.

There are so many beautiful men and women here.

Cukor gives me a dismissive glance that tells me I'm ridic-
ulously out of place in this crowd, maybe it's these chukka-
style shoes, God knows they set me back.

Farley Granger or Guy Haines or whoever he is returns
with that off-center grin. "Now I get it. You're a fan. Very
déclassé around here, but I love it. Stick around if you like.
Food and drinks."

I'm tempted but instead retreat toward the wall gate
where I bump into a big well-muscled guy in slacks, sandals,
and a preppy short-sleeve button-down shirt.

Radovan Kovacs.

Ray looks spectacular, as usual, the handsomest man I
know. Chiseled face, eyes to dream for, strong affirmative
jaw, high hard "Indian" cheekbones, power-lifter's deltoids,
a permanent beach tan. Rory Calhoun over there by the
pool should look this good.

"Ray?" I tap him on the back.

He turns, and his face flushes under the tan.

He grabs my elbow, hey that hurts, and steers me over
to a private corner under a jacaranda tree where we stumble
over each other in chorus: "What are you doing here?"

It's been months since his "trial" in Panorama City.

He looks around for eavesdroppers and then it all comes
tumbling out in a barely coherent stream of words:

". . . *majka mrtva* . . . can you fucking believe it? . . .
zajebati Russians . . ." His words rattle out like bullets, the
news that his mother collapsed of a heart attack during her
weekly trip to the Soviet consulate to plead for the release of
her older son from a Russian gulag.

Ray's eyes dust up as he wipes away angry tears. "Fuck fuck fuck all that . . . do you want my books?. . . . I'm throwing them out . . . Little Lenin Library all that shit. I'm into the good stuff . . . Comic strips . . . that's where the reality is . . . *Alley Oop* and *Terry and the Pirates*, you have no idea what L'il Abner is really saying . . . it's all in code . . . you just have to decipher it . . . next time you see me I'm in a suit and tie . . . they'll never find me . . . fuck going to med school I'll work for Xerox or IBM . . ."

I step back from his verbal fury and put my hands on his shoulders to get him to slow down.

He looks at me straight. "Don't do that unless you mean it," he says of my bracing him.

I do mean it, I insist.

He says, "I mean mean it."

Involuntary recoil. Back away like an unseen hand pushes me. A mere flick of a reflex. A vast pale dismay spreads over Ray's lovely face, and that wonderful jaw sets like granite. I don't know where to put my hands, we're so used to manhandling each other.

I make it worse by insisting: "But you won a letter on the wrestling team!"

Now that's really stupid.

Images: Ray dive-bombing to defecate out of the Piper Cub; Ray's pure joy in bar brawls; Ray pranking the FBI with his "I'm Boris the Russian spy" act . . . my God we've shared the same beach blanket and slept together under it . . . even in the same bed. Who knew? An electrical storm goes off in my head.

What was it Terry once told me that I laughed off? "You and Ray are two of a kind and I saved you." Saved, from what? I'm not walking down that road.

Secondhand feelings that grow from movies instead of a living heart rescue me from what I really want to do, which is put my arms around Ray and tell him it's going to be okay because once he had my back and I'll have his from now on. An involuntary image from *Double Indemnity* suppresses real emotion: the dying insurance salesman Fred MacMurray confesses to his boss, Edward G. Robinson, that Robinson was unable to solve the murder case because the killer was too close to him, right across the desk. "Closer than that," Robinson says. "I love you, too," whispers MacMurray.

I love Radovan Kovacs. Loved him. Oh shit, I don't know.

I step back from the heat of his furious disappointment.

". . . And, you know what? The Sunday color comics tell us all what we need to know. Why didn't you tell me? *Pogo* and *Brenda Starr* . . ."

He's kidding, no?

He's serious, yes. He quotes Pogo the comic possum, "'We have met the enemy—and he is us.' Top that!"

When did the enemy become us and not them?

"I'm through with the Movement." Now his arm sweeps out toward the pool, "And with them, too."

"Them" is . . . ? I scan the crowd and all I see are film stars at leisure.

He risks putting his hands on my shoulder and turns me toward the crowd around the pool.

"Dummy," he murmurs into my ear. "Look. I'm only here because I'm pretty."

Ah. So. Yes. Got it. Dummy, dummy me.

❖

RAY IS TO blame for my split lip. His absence in my life forces me to trawl bars alone. Ohh, my head hurts. What made me ask the guy at the next table if he plucked his eyebrows? Ah, Ray. For a minute it was like the old days until I hit the floor.

He shouldn't have done this to me.

❖

TERRY SAYS, "RAY called you dumb? Wrong. You're stupid. You bought his story about the Air Force kicking him out because of his politics. Think about it. Why else do they discharge a man?"

50

A Star Is Born

Janet Gaynor (as Esther Blodgett): Some day you won't laugh at me! I'm going out and have a real life! I'm gonna be somebody!

—From *A Star Is Born* (1937); writers Dorothy Parker and Ring Lardner Jr. are blacklisted

M IDNIGHT AT THE Andalusia Gardens, alone and typing, over and over again, "'*Do you feel better?*' *he asked. 'I feel fine,' she said. 'There's nothing wrong with me. I feel fine.*'" End. Start over. "*The hill across the valley of the Ebro . . .*"

A soft knock on my open screen door on a warm night. "Hey there, Clancy, compadre, I hear you in there working on the Great American novel," young Jeff the FBI man announces through the wire mesh.

I feared they'd forgotten me.

Strange guy. Solo again. Where does Jeff come off pretending he hadn't tried to kill me by running my car off the Pacific Coast Highway when his date with Anita went south? Tonight he's changed his standard government-issue uniform of bad-taste sports coat, white shirt, conservative tie, pressed cuffed pants, and shined shoes for Wild One chic, denim jeans, a black T-shirt, and moccasins. Weapon under his T-shirt?

In a practiced move he eases in with his small, angry eyes X-raying the room.

"What can I do for you, kemo sabe?" I ask.

Prowling, he approaches to stroke my turtle Buddy then thinks better of it and occupies his usual canvas-covered chair across from me.

"A drink?" he asks.

This is a surprise.

"There's only White Horse."

"Straight. No water. Please."

Please yet. Mormon manners.

As I'm in the kitchen pouring, I look out the window to see if the yellow Chevy is parked outside.

Then we raise our dime-store Coca-Cola glasses to each other. "Happier days," I say.

"God bless America," he replies, then sighs deeply.

"I'm sorry about Dale," he stares into his Scotch. No shame these guys. Dale, an elementary school teacher and comrade, tired of the fears we all feel, lay down in his bathtub with a razor blade but not before leaving a note for his children on the locked door: DO NOT OPEN. CALL THE POLICE.

Bastards.

Jeff says, "Can you do a screen test of me?"

He is joking. But not.

He follows up, "I'd pay for your time. Or for the camera-man, whatever it takes."

I say, you tried to kill me. His look says, Come on, grow up.

Does madness run in the FBI family?

He is serious. A screen test. Next stop for him, Atascadero State Hospital.

But wait. Play along with his fantasy that I have Hollywood power. Maybe I do.

Yes.s.s.s . . . in a certain light . . . depends on angle, that stub-like square stone face has . . . possibilities. A college wrestler's build, like Ray. True, he's no six-footer but look at the box-office $8 million on rentals on Alan Ladd's *Shane* at five-foot-five! My fallen angel–agent takes over as I square my fingers to frame him as a photomontage of body parts belonging to Audie Murphy, Tab Hunter, Rory Calhoun, and George Hamilton.

Name change? What is his real name anyway?

He pretends to read a book from the shelf, and mumbles. How's that?

"Artennis Wilford Kimball."

"Artemis? Like in *The Three Musketeers*?"

He spells it out, uncomfortably. "A-r-t-e-double n-i-s."

Yes, I can do this! If the industry can swallow Tab, Race, Rock, Troy, and all the other Tom of Finland porno-poster *noms de cinema*, why not, er, um, let's see, think fast, Buzz, Buzz Jeffrey, no Buzz Hoover, no Buzz Law. That's it!

Buzz Law.

Scotches on top of the Tuinal-plus-Dexxies may impair
my judgment, but clear as day I can picture dragging Buzz
Law into the office as the next . . . the next . . . well, the next
. . . Buzz Law. Take that, James Dean!

Jeff, without irony, "I'd really appreciate it. You're the
only subject I know in the movie business." This guy is as
screwed up as I am.

He smiles for the first time—oh, must fix those teeth,
maybe a little jawline work.

He reaches behind into his belt and pulls out not a gun
but a manila envelope and hands it over: inside are headshots of himself.

Downstairs somebody honks.

He reaches over to retrieve his headshots, changes and
rechanges his mind, finally deposits the manila envelope
back on my coffee table.

He looks at me. "Thanks a lot, my friend."

He knows me better than I know myself.

❖

IT WOULD BE feathers in my cap to bring in a fresh new
actor like my protégé Buzz Law. But there I go distracting
myself from the prosaic part of my job, policing writers'
contracts to make sure they're on the job and deliver their
scripts on time.

51

How to Break
a Writer's Block

ONE OF MICKEY Cohen's several side businesses
helps Jaffe writer-clients finish their screenplays by
literally screwing it out of them. Luckily, his upscale house
of ill repute in the hills above our office is patrolled by LA
County sheriffs who are even more bribable than LAPD.
Jaffe screenwriters have the privilege of enjoying, gratis, this
brothel managed by Cohen's two girlfriends on condition
the writer produces to strict deadline. (We have no similar
arrangement with women writers.)

Example: the breezy, talented, and high-priced Boston-
based "Brian McIntyre" is married with kids, chronically
late on his assignments and a serial pussy lover not necessar-
ily that of his wife's. When we secure for him his highest paid
job to date—$1,500 a week on a twelve-week guarantee at
Metro—the deadline passes without a completed screenplay.
Holed up at the Garden of Allah, Brian drinks but doesn't
write until, finally fed up, Mary calls in her chips. "Principal

photography starts next week. They need his script now, not *spaeter*. Kidnap the sonofabitch if you have to."

On a Friday Ace, Zack, and I bundle Brian from his hotel room and dump him at the front door of a Neutra-style flat-roofed modernistic house in a cul-de-sac at the end of one of the canyon roads where a moonlighting deputy sheriff, in uniform, one of Mickey's employees, takes over. The following Monday I alone drive up into the hills where I'm led into a messy, blinds-drawn bedroom to McIntyre, in pajamas, one leg shackled to the unmade bed, at a desk pounding a typewriter as if it's his enemy. Brian, normally shaved and suited as befits a Princeton man—he and Jonny Buck are classmates—is shaggy haired and looks like Alley Oop the cartoon caveman, his eyes burning bright. The deputy remarks, "We feed him on the hour. Every ten pages he gets a blowjob if he wants one."

End of story: Brian produces his script on time and returns home to wife and hearth exhausted, drained, and richer by $20,000 plus.

The system works.

52

The Defiant Ones

I ain't mad . . . I been mad all my natural life.

—Sidney Poitier in *The Defiant Ones* (1958), cowritten by
blacklisted Nedrick Young under a false name. Embarrassingly,
it wins an Academy Award for best screenplay.

AN OLD JOKE:
*A lost soul wanders into a western saloon pleading,
"Gimme a drink and hurry. I've been walkin' in the desert
for days." The bartender flings off his apron and runs away,
"Help yourself. Big Ed is coming!" The stranger starts to
pour himself a drink when he hears the thump-thump-
THUMP! of approaching hobnail boots. His hand freezes
halfway to his parched lips. The saloon door swings open.
The stranger's eyes widen to take the full measure of the
newcomer who is a giant of a man. "D-d-do you want a d-d-
d-drink?" the little guy tremblingly offers his glass. The huge
man shakes his head. "Ain't got time," the monster rumbles,
"Big Ed is coming!"*

My Big Ed she is coming on fast.

❖

SCENE: MY PRIVATE office overlooking the Strip. The mid-day sun angles in like a kamikaze and slams into the white cement sidewalks below. I stare down at the street pretending to be a sniper—I'm infantry trained on the M84 scoped Springfield .03 sighted for 2,500 yards point blank at 200 yards—picking off a two-man target in fedoras just sitting there at the curb in a Chevy Coupe. In this heat.

Terry Allison, former Tova Abramovitch, enters without knocking.

Surprised, I turn away from my sniper station. "How did you get past Joanna and Addy?" I ask.

"Told them I'm your best fuck. Did I lie?" A strange thing about Terry; she'll shout and scream, punch and kick, but until now will never use that word. Raised decently.

Her habit of tightlipped orgasms, eyes rolling up into her head showing only the whites, like the blind stare of the ambulatory dead man in *I Walked With a Zombie*, stupifies and turns me on. After sex we are strangers to each other. Until now I believed that was the deal memo between us.

For privacy I close the door.

"I need for us to talk," Terry says.

She's never been to the office. Strict limits. She doesn't come here, and I don't butt into her cutting room where she is in charge of laying a Laff Track on the Groucho Marx show, *You Bet Your Life*.

She's pregnant?

She shakes her head, on the verge of tears.

Then, what? Not feeling well?

"Isn't my period, either or does your little Jewish puritanism cringe at my bodily cycle? You don't seem to mind the rest of the month."

"Ter—."

"It's Terry. You never call me my name. Not ever!"

A declaration of war, she's never spoken to me like this before.

Terry: "Boy, do you look scared. I want to talk about our relationship." What?

Until now we mocked couples who indulge in re-la-tion-ship babble.

Come on, Ter . . . Terry.

"Let's get married," she demands. She looks hesitant. "Will you?"

What?

"You fool, you love me. I think I love you. What else have we been doing with each other?" Her voice weakens. "Why not?" She adds, "We're not what we think we are but what we do. Don't you see that? We have free will. Existentially."

Where is this coming from? She hasn't been quite herself since the Feds, we guess it's them, arranged her car accident on Melrose, overturning her Mercury. And that night, perversely, we had the best sex ever over her bruised body.

In my office, she stands to smooth her wide wool skirt. Smashing figure. "Obviously," she says, "you don't want to talk about us. Will you ever grow up?"

I stall for time. "Um, where do you get all this . . . Terry?"

"Simone de Beauvoir, that's who!" she shoots back.

"Who?"

She strides to the door, turns, and makes a small pirouette like a model (which she's been), faces me with one long-fingered hand on her hip, and smiles for the first time. Wickedly.

"*The Second Sex*—" here she put both hands on her hips defiantly. "Le Deuxième Sexe."

"Is there a movie in it?"

She starts to sweep out, then deflates. "Go ahead. Make a joke. I know you can outtalk me. But . . . but . . ." she loses the trail. Then perks up. "Simone de Beauvoir says . . . says . . ."

When she breaks down crying I go to comfort her, but she raises her hands as if fending off Dracula. Venomous and exalted, she shouts: "I DON'T NEED YOU TO TELL ME I AM A WOMAN!"

She sniffles. "I was born a—no, that's not right. I was not born a woman, I'm becoming one . . ." She bites her lip. "Okay, so I don't get it right the first time. But I know what I mean."

"I know you do," I say, soothingly.

Through the tears she throws me a look of pure murder. "NO YOU DON'T—dumb schmuck." And storms out.

Something weird and unprecedented is happening out there. Curious, I drive down to Hollywood Boulevard's Larry Edmunds bookstore to check out the photograph on the dust jacket of this French female writer who has upset Terry. And then meet my client Nelson Algren for coffee and Danish on the Strip.

"Nelson, who is this Bo-var mamzelle?"

"They'll love your accent in Paris," Nelson replies.

Nelson, the Chicago-bred novelist, and I are taking the sun under an awning outside the diner on the Strip a few doors down from the agency. Mary Baker bequeathed Algren to me after Otto Preminger bought his novel *The Man With the Golden Arm* and screwed him, over money and with serious discourtesy, with our help because the agency preferred to keep the good will of a powerful producer to that of a tramp poet. "Find work for the poor slob, keep him company, get him a girl, anything," Mary commanded.

My assignment is to make a National Book Award author feel good about having been betrayed by almost everyone he comes in contact with in Hollywood, including his agents. Nelson doesn't blame me personally (he says). I hadn't made the original bad deal for him, but to compensate I work doubly hard to get him a paying job. (Warners exec: "Our respect for you, Mister Algren, is insurmountable. We have this project about a nun who falls in love with a tennis player . . . We call it *Jumping the Net*.") Nelson is a proud, angry, generous man and mainly we spend our time together talking Chicago baseball; both of us dreamed of playing in the majors. Over coffee I ramble on about Simone Bo-var's photo on the book jacket. "You ever run across her in Paris?" Maybe one day, I boast, I'll go to France and see if I can be a writer, too. The surprising words are out of my mouth before I know it, I'm just trying it on for size.

He shuts his eyes against the sun. Nelson's love affair with the feminist author is immortalized in her novel *The*

Mandarins, but is unknown to me because these days all I read are scripts for sale and packaging.

So I buy my own copies of *The Second Sex* because of its jacket photo of the lady in a Lana Turner turban, and then, stupidly, in a brainstorm of didactic enthusiasm, circulate the books among the Ladies Auxiliary so that we're all on the same page, literally.

They react variously.

Laura, the old woman at thirty-four, dying before my eyes of what turns out to be leukemia, slaps me upside the head with the bulky book, demonstrating a passion she has never before indicated in or out of the Tiffany wicker chaise longue in which she insists we make love. Chain-smoking B-Jay, the fashion writer, who after sex hops up and down to expel my sperm, chucks Beauvoir into a wastebasket with a toss of her aquiline head and a contemptuous tap of ash from her cigarette holder. "Hah! You hypocrite!" Rhoda, the lady weightlifter, says, "Second what?" Multilingual Van, MGM contract actress, has already read Beauvoir in the original and so what else is new? Annie, the factory girl who bounces me up and down in bed like a Spaldeen, is embarrassed because, I now learn, she cannot read. Petra, the ninety-five-pound Lewitzky dancer driving in from her husband's bed to mine at midnight and back home before sunrise, flips through the pages with such interest that before leaving my place in the morning she forgets to have sex. Kelly, UCLA homecoming princess, divorced mother of two, asks "Does Beauvoir say anything about how to raise kids?" Maggie, the black librarian who votes Republican, is outraged at Beauvoir's comparison of women's to black oppression. And Bobette, the Rand numbers cruncher with the eyelid infirmity, snarls, "Thanks for nothing" and, like Laura, hurls the book at me.

Until now they brushed aside my pamphlets as a minor abnormality, like coming too fast or daydreaming during their orgasms. But now . . .

They lay an ambush.

Laura, on crutches, invites me to lunch at Musso & Frank, and while we're at the counter with the corned beef and cabbage special, slyly suggests a more comfortable move to a booth in the main dining room, where—surprise!—await Van, Renata, B-Jay, Rhoda, Bobette, and Kelly. No Terry.

I'm trapped by their massed glares. Apparently B-Jay and Rhoda bumped into each other at the bookstore when they returned the book for cash, and it escalated from there.

Laura, showing surprising strength in a fatally ill woman, drags me bodily into the middle of the group in the booth. "Thanks for coming," Kelly, the glossy, all-American girl, says. "You patronizing bastard." Bobette gets right to the point. "You're a mess, Clancy." She should talk, showing zero interest in me until I got beat up in a fight and the hospital bandaged me like the Invisible Man and from then on, even after I healed, she could only do it if my face was wrapped in gauze. And I'm the mess?

Petra says, "You should get help for your problem."

"What we rezent," offers Van, with her faint Viennese accent like Peter Lorre, "iz zat you treat uz like idiots."

"How," demands small-boned Petra, "can you imagine we would not find out about all the others?"

The possibility never entered my mind.

"Horseshit," spits Rhoda. "You're nothing but a burned-out case. Where do you get the energy to lock us in all those secret compartments?" Is this my intellectually challenged, high school dropout cocksucking Rhoda?

So you guys have read my Beauvoir after all? I ask. I pronounce her name correctly now.

A table full of women roll their eyes to heaven. His Beauvoir.

B-Jay leans toward me until her powdered nose practically touches mine. "All this time you thought you were using us, we were using you."

My mother Jennie warned me. Always listen to your mom.

Kelly: "Know what's so sad? You have all these Big Noble Thoughts, liberating this and protesting that, and they have nothing to do with your life, you're a zombie with a prick."

Rhoda says, "We thought you weren't like other guys. Wrong, you're worse."

The arrogance of these women, whom I didn't seek out but got referred to as you'd find a painless dentist.

Kelly says, "We know you laid three of us in one day. That's sick."

Laura tells the women, "Have to give him one thing. He never asked us 'Was it good for you?'"

"Of courze not!" says Van. "He hazn't a clue. Handz up, who faked coming?"

Five hands pop up, they exchange looks and all seven burst into laughter.

Now it's my turn to be angry.

Laura says to Rhoda, "You know, he's right. We're not his doctor."

"Absolutely," I say, primly. "How many men you know who take your brains as seriously as I do?"

Raucous laughter all round. Laura, "He may have a point. Like his penis a small point, but still."

I start to squirm out of the horseshoe-shaped booth and am pushed back by Rhoda. "We're not through with you yet." A controlled panic works through my system.

Kelly, "I'm curious. Did you actually read the book you gave us?"

"Twice," I lie.

Van, "He's impozzible. Look at him. Let him go, he'z ruining my lunch."

Seven against one, the odds are not in my favor. What would Hemingway do? Did John Reed have this problem with Louise Bryant or Henry Miller with Anaïs Nin? Or Frank with Ava?

B-Jay, who seems to hold a grudge against herself for sleeping with me, bridles as always. "He's a condescending sonofabitch."

Van sobers me up. "Maybe you did, maybe you didn't, rezpect our brains. But you didn't liberate uz, we liberated you. You were all cramped up when we found you. Yes, we found you. You are a much better lover now zan before." She turns to the other women for validation but none of them nod in agreement. An ego crusher.

"Hey ladies," I say, "What do you want? My head, my balls, a written confession signed in my blood?"

B-Jay says, "For starters."

❖

DIMLY I SUSPECT my future may no longer include Laura, Bobette, Petra, Rhoda, Kelly, B-Jay, and Vanessa.

Laura releases me by laying aside her crutches.

Once escaped in the aisle I try a face-saving gesture.

"Ladies," I bow.

As with one voice they protest: "WOMEN!"

Oh, shit, Big Ed is here.

PART SEVEN

53

Death of a Salesman

"WHAT ARE YOUR plans?" Mary Baker asks, sipping from her normal Bloody Mary. This time I join her.

I laugh uncomfortably. "I'm not going anywhere."

Mary says, "Yes you are. It's written all over you. For months. Clients notice."

Defensive. "Any complaints?"

"Yes, mine." she replies. "I can't see blood on your teeth anymore."

I'm silent.

"Think it over, kid. This ain't a business for old men."

Used to be. Look at agent Sam Jaffe and other active sacred monsters like 73-year-old Louis Mayer, 83-year-old Adolph Zukor, Skouras at 63, 65-year-old Harry Cohn, etc. But now all those crazy, intuition-driven old men are dying off or being elbowed out. I'm losing fathers. True, even as they donated to American-Jewish causes they crawled for Hitler's favor so as not to lose the German market. None of them, with the possible exception of Carl Laemmle, lifted a finger to protest when the Nazis fired Jewish employees of the German film industry. Until Pearl Harbor they even let Hitler's agents, including LA's Nazi consul, have veto power over film content. Hypocrites and cowards with a touch of cruel genius.

Today's studio executives are no longer ex-vaudeville hoofers and pushcart peddlers, but the Smooth Young Men with college degrees, versions of Terry's unctuous Dr. Mark, less vulgar, better educated, and gutless.

Mary's office grows quieter inside and out as people pack up to go home. It's the best time of the day, when the typewriters cease their rifle fire, high heels on hardwood floors go silent, and lights are switched off one by one. On warm smogless nights I lever-open my office window and take in all of the LA flatlands clear out to the ocean, a view that beckons me to come body surfing with Ray, who is no longer part of my life or maybe his own either.

The outer workstations are deserted, agents and secretaries gone, even the janitor Washington has left. In her office Mary and I sit quietly, separated only by the distance of her Persian antique carpet, neither of us saying anything. It's quitting time, sweet and solemn.

Through her half-open French-plum drapes I can see the sun setting way out over the palm trees near the airport.

There's a wall bench between her desk and my chair. I loosen my tie, and she—amazing, she hardly ever does it—removes her hat, tonight a 1920s cloche number, usually tipped over one eye. She inserts a Pall Mall in her bone ivory cigarette holder, and I say, "No." She puts the cigarette back in her inlaid silver case.

I go sit by the bench. Mary doesn't move.

She shrugs out of her tailored white-pique bolero jacket and lets it drop to the floor. She's wearing an off-white silk blouse with a silly little bow at the throat, and comes over to sit next to me at the wall bench. I reach over to untie the silly bow, let the two ends hang down, take out my pocket handkerchief and, very slowly, wipe off the broad slash of red lipstick, something I've wanted to do since my first day. She's much better looking without makeup, which I tell her.

Hoarsely, she replies, "You'll have me naked yet."

Button by button, I undo her silk blouse but don't take it off, and we sit there, in near darkness.

Her phone rings. She's half undressed. It stops ringing, then starts again. Two rings, pause, two more.

Mary says, "Bogie."

Without bothering to button up she rises and picks up the phone, listens, says "I'll be there," and hangs up.

She tells me, "In the hospital. Under the knife."

I didn't even know he was sick. She replies, "Then you haven't seen his last two pictures. Don't you go to the movies any more?"

She and Sam Jaffe have been Bogart's agents for twenty years, going back to when Bogart's third wife, Mayo Methot, stabbed him in the back with a kitchen knife, and his first call was to his agents, not a doctor or paramedics. Sam has made all of his deals, some good some bad, and through all the domestic dramas and fights over scripts and brawls with directors and big money offers from other agents, they've come through together.

I help her button up and put on her bolero jacket just right. She goes into the small bathroom off her office to reapply that blazing red lipstick, fix her hair, and scrutinize her reflection in the small mirror. "I've been gray since I was fifteen. Do you think I should cut it shorter? Page boy like Judith Anderson?"

Judith Anderson. Click.

Mary putting her mask back on in the bathroom: "She's the Queen of Kvetch, we got DeMille to pay her a fortune for a minute's work in *The Ten Commandments*. Paramount's cash built her that house in Santa Barbara, I keep telling her Santa Barbara is for rich lesbian hermits, and she says takes one to know one."

She comes out of the bathroom, Mary Baker, powerful agent.

She says, "Bogie's dying. Everyone in town knows except him. When he goes I'm outta here. What about you?"

Where thou goest I go, I want to say. This remarkable woman taught me the business, paid for my mistakes, cooled my panics, celebrated my triumphs and stomped on me as a teaching tool, fought off the wolves, gave me undeserved raises, and not least fired up in me the inescapable hots for a gray-haired women fifteen years my senior who's left me hanging over a precipice of gratitude and lust.

Ever since I came on this job Mary and I, by some miracle of chemistry, have been tuned into each other. We know the other person's way of communicating without speaking. A raised eyebrow, flick of an ash, a certain tone.

I can see it coming.

Just before she goes out to Bogart's house, Mary turns to me. "We'll miss you, Kid."

I've just been fired.

❖

NO COUNTRY FOR OLD MEN NO MATTER HOW YOUNG WE ARE

Bogie's death draws a final curtain on Sam and Mary's and my era of filmmaking. The future no longer belongs to Stanwyck, Bette and Joan, Gable, Cagney and Flynn but to Brando, Clift and Steiger, Grace and Kim and Natalie; and to younger polished executives, and to agents like me, harbinger of a new kind of huckster, college-educated and sterile. If not careful, I'm destined for success.

That night when I go out on my balcony overlooking the Spanish fountain, all is strangely quiet at the Andalusia. The evening smells of jasmine and burnt cinders from backyard incinerators. The driveway downstairs is clear of strange federal cars, the street lamp I broke to obscure their vision is still unrepaired, trust the LA Department of Water and Power. Night sounds echo around the neighborhood.

In the apartment I pick up the phone, which has no familiar static, unscrew it to examine the receiver, and poke around the walls for an extra bug. I peer under the couch, chairs, rattan carpet, at the light fixtures, anywhere a transmitter can be hidden, and find nothing. I'm clean.

Like Ray, the FBI has vanished from my life.

I needed villains in my life, and now they're gone. The only villain left is myself.

54

The Long Goodbye

O MENS. MY BELOVED turtle Buddy is gone. He escaped from his orange box when the balcony door was open. I looked all over the apartment and neighborhood but nothing. Where do Mojave turtles go?

At the office Addy is weeping. Tears drip onto her notebook where she scribbles notes in longhand because she never learned Pitman, Gregg, or even Speed Writing.

I hand her a Kleenex. She sighs.

"What will I tell anyone who calls?"

"I've gone fishing."

"You're so cruel. Where are you going, what will you do?"

"You sound like my mother."

Real anxiety: "And all your clients?"

Mary Baker is parceling them out among the platoon, and I've held grief sessions with the mutts who Zack has agreed to take on in exchange for my promise to toss his wife's .38 in the Pacific.

Peter Lorre I've failed yet again because we forced him to work on *Congo Crossing*, a disease story in the mythical African kingdom of Congotanga, shooting in the LA Botanic Gardens in Arcadia near Santa Anita racetrack.

Farewell, my lovelies.

At Warner Brothers for the last time I check in on my contract writers, including an alcoholic script doctor for whom I smuggle in Thermoses of vodka martinis to keep him at the typewriter. Walter Isaacs, now with MCA, says Jack Warner likes the end I wrote for him. "Do I get a credit?" I ask, and he says, "Not even in jest, please."

Over at Universal the late morning is alive with the sounds of hammering, teamsters' shouts, the whine of saws and four-wheel electric vehicles. Carl Laemmle's old studio may be financially shaky—they haven't bought anything from me for weeks—but the place is still humming. As usual, I like to climb and hide in the rafters to spy on the practical gods manhandling the physical apparatus of movie making—heavy lights, stanchions, cameras, dolly tracks— so beautifully solid and real, not like my evanescent deals and lies that go uncaught.

How can I ever leave all this?

I hate abandoning Abbott and Costello where *Dance With Me, Henry* has a dying Costello and Bud Abbott a pale shadow of his scrawnier self. This has to be their last film together, and they don't look as if they'll get through it. On the next set over is the finale of the Ma & Pa Kettle series, without (alas) Percy Kilbride as Pa; there's some new Pa I never heard of.

"Miss Main," I say, "where's Mister Kilbride?"

Marjorie's friend Miss Byington looks up from her flashing needles. "Oh, isn't that too bad," she responds brightly. "We have no idea why the studio replaced him."

"Horse manure. Don't be such a hypocrite," Main cackles as she makes a circling motion with index finger to her head. "Gaga. Heck of a thing to see."

Byington says primly, "You're a minister's daughter and should pray for him."

Main slaps my knee, "Too late for that, right, sonny boy!"

Finally, over on Stage 8, what luck! My second favorite fiend, the Gill-Man, is shooting *The Creature Walks Among Us*, producer Bill Alland's sequel to *The Creature From the Black Lagoon*. Perverse man, Alland is shooting a script from a soon-to-be blacklisted writer, Arthur Ross, one of the several leftists Alland always seems to be drawn to.

Alland spots me watching today's scene where the maddened Gill-Man goes berserk in his cage. "Hear you're leaving us," he doesn't even bother to glance up from his clipboard while scrutinizing how his set is dressed.

The director summons Gill-Man to the set and I watch the last surviving member of a race of amphibious humanoids accidentally trip over some breakaway furniture, causing Alland, ever conscious of budget, to reluctantly order a reshoot. I'd like to hang around but Alland kisses me off. "You should have taken my offer, we would have made a great team. Now you're yesterday's man, kid. Off my set."

What else did I expect? Friendship?

Outside in the sunlit studio alley Alland catches up with me and tugs at my sleeve. "I could have turned you in. But you served your country in time of war and didn't stay home like the rest of your swimming pool comrades," and goes back inside the soundstage, another creature who walks among us.

As I'm exiting the lot I pass the open door of an editing cubicle and see "Karl Belson" bent over a Movieola splicing film, his wrists still bandaged almost to the elbow.

Karl was a Red friend who, under pressure, razor-slashed himself.

"What are you doing here?" we ask each other. With a slightly hunted look he firmly takes my arm out of the editing room and down the alley where he can light up.

"So, comrade . . ." he grins.

I'm an agent, he's a film editor, and we've beaten the blacklist, for now. Unspoken: Whom did we inform on to keep our jobs?

"I'm getting married next week," he announces.

Mazel tov.

"She knows nothing about me so don't come to the wedding."

Did he cave? He knows I want to know. He stubs out his cigarette under his shoe and says he has to get back to work. Without even saying goodbye he heads back down the alley, jauntily swinging his bandaged arms.

"Hey, Karl," I say.

He's almost running now.

"What are you working on?" I yell.

Just as he ducks back into his editing room, he looks back at me:

"*Revenge of the Creature.*"

55

The Non-Union Indian

Harry Landers (as Grey Wolf): There can be no friendship between Red Man and White. The fight is to the end.

—From *The Indian Fighter* (1955); writer Robert Richards is blacklisted and becomes a carpenter

T HE LAST STOP on my goodbye tour is Republic Pictures, that pearl of easy-access studios, cheapest of the majors and home to authentic picture making, Gene Autry, Roy Rogers, and the dozen mind-bending chapters of *Daredevils of the Red Circle*.

You made me what I am today.

Unlike swankier lots like Fox and Metro, which have Fort Knox–like security, all you do at Republic is saunter past a snoozing guard. Just to hang around the Republic movie-making machine is to absorb a post-grad course in "cinema" by paying attention to its stable of veteran directors, like the incredible Joe Kane who on-the-trot shoots eight or nine movies a year, though age has slowed him down to two or three. (Take that, Orson Welles, George

Cukor, and William Wyler!) Joe will film the telephone directory if you hand him a dollar and a Mitchell camera. Kane is used to seeing me putzing around his sets, today a cop drama with the world's worst actress, the studio boss's sleep-in sweetheart, Czech ice skater Vera Hrubá Ralston, yodeling as a nightclub singer. Kane, checking for sound, takes off his headphones and hands them to me. "Let's print this scene and put her out of her misery, okay?"

I love wandering along Suburban Street and Hacienda Square (by turns an Alamo fort, Tombstone jailhouse, or Mexican cantina) and on down to the Radford Avenue dead end at the Los Angeles trickle of a river where old props like cardboard dinosaur heads and tinplate flying saucers from *Radar Men from the Moon* are dumped on the sloping cement banks.

Just beyond the river there's an "Indian" village with an encampment of Screen Actors Guild warriors and their squaws, looking suspiciously Japanese or Chinese, taking a break.

A pistol crack wakes me up. "You there! In my shot! Asswise move!"

The assistant director, a pug in a baseball cap, points a starter's gun at me across the stream.

I wave good-naturedly, but gun in hand the A.D. splashes across to ask if I want to make ten bucks "off the books" because the scene is shy of a paleface.

Sure, my time is your time.

The A.D. says they're in a hurry so please take off all my clothes except the Jockey shorts and recross the dry riverbed with him, where on the other side, the script girl rolls up my jacket and trousers, shoes and socks, and swears she'll protect the bundle with her life. While the director assembles the fake Indians for a long shot, the A.D. ties a chamois loincloth around my middle and leads me to the center of the movie village and spread-eagles me on the ground and ties both my wrists and ankles to wooden pegs.

The boss director, who wears a stained bush hat and looks as if he's been making movies since William S. Hart, strolls over. "Okay, you, squirm! Wiggle your tush in agony. But no dialogue. Not even a burp or SAG will have a shit-fit." He climbs a trestle chair to oversee the scene. "All right, Indians—hoochie koochie, war dance! Camera! Sound!"

The A.D. explains, "The chief's son will slice up your white renegade heart."

Oh great. A broad-chested brave hovers with upraised Bowie knife aimed at my aorta. I shut my eyes, this is a movie, right?

"Action!"

The warrior hurls atop my nearly naked paleface body, Oof! Something grazes my side.

"Cut! Print!"

My Apache tormentor rolls off and pretends to wipe my blood off the easily bendable blade.

Alone on the ground, I yell for someone to cut me loose and give me back my clothes, but no one is paying attention.

Well, look at it this way. On *Bride of the Gorilla* I began my career as a lesser breed in back of the camera. Now I'm in front of it.

That's progress.

56

Mojave Green

T HE AGENCY OWES me two weeks' paid final vacation, which I take driving a rented Plymouth Belvedere toward the rising sun on Highway 80 through Tombstone to the Llano Estacado out near Odessa and the Panhandle and Southern Oklahoma, to pursue an obsession with the life and death of the great Comanche chief Quanah Parker, who never lost a battle to the white man, surrendering on his own terms, his Quehada tribe of Comanches the last to come in. Obsession means reading everything about him I can lay my hands on.

Day after day in the broiling Southwest sun I walk and drive all over the Staked Plains, visiting battle sites and listening on their front porches to elderly men, who claim to have been Texas Rangers, reminisce, or lie, about fighting Indians on the frontier. Quanah's mother Cynthia was a captive white woman, Prairie Flower his half white sister; on Quanah's death, he gave instructions for his burial next to them at Fort Sill military cemetery, and I get out of the Plymouth to lay a bouquet of Texas bluebells on their marked graves.

Quanah, an expert horseman and warrior, has long fascinated me because of his intense relationship with his mother Jennie I mean Cynthia and what must have been his most agonizing dilemma, whether or not he and his tribe should die fighting to the last man, woman, and child—or save themselves by giving in to the whites. On the lonely escarpments I can hear him arguing with himself: Should I survive in the mainstream and thus die spiritually, or fight to a quick and noble death? I identify to the point of fixation.

On returning to LA, I sit at my Corona portable and pound out a screenplay based on Quanah, which the Jaffe agents unanimously reject as pathetic—plus the "Indian thing" is on its way out, and anyway our client Ray Danton is already cast as Chief Crazy Horse, in a pinch there's always Victor Mature, Lex Barker, and even Boris Karloff but it doesn't occur to any of us to suggest a real Indian to play Quanah Parker. Authentic Comanches and Apaches never play leads but dutifully tumble off their horses on the near side of the camera after John Wayne plugs them with a single bullet.

SORRY, QUANAH.

I forget all about him until the July evening when, for the last time, my FBI spook Jeff, alias Buzz Law the next Tab Hunter, shows up on my back porch.

He does his usual wandering around the living room, commiserates on my loss of Buddy and browses through my books, noticing several I've been using as Comanche research.

"You into Indians?" Leafing pages, "I'm half. Well, a quarter. To be honest, I don't know, maybe one-sixteenth. Shoshone but my people intermarried with the Bannock and Utes up where I was raised."

"I thought you were Mormon."

"Am. RM. Returned Missionary. 'Go ye therefore and teach all nations.' Matthew 28. When they drove us into Fort Hall, some of the clan drifted south to join up with the Utes to fight the Cheyenne, and when General Howard practically wiped us out, one thing led to another, relationshipwise with whites."

"Your boss knows all this?" I ask. Famously, FBI has no minority agents.

"Director Hoover loves Mormons. He knows how we suffered for our religion. Calls us his Young Commandos for Freedom."

He flips pages of my Indian books. "All marked up," Jeff says. "You really into it?"

So there we are, chatting away about our mutual interest in the first Americans, and don't ask me how this happens, but that weekend, in his and my spare time, in his big Dodge Meadowbrook—a family car, is he married?—we drive into the Mojave Desert, home of my vanished turtle Buddy, looking for stray Indian heads. It's a male bonding thing, especially when he draws out his service revolver and blows the head off what he says is a Mojave Green rattlesnake about to strike me outside Bullhead City. Blam! The snake's head flies off, and I go to retrieve it. Maybe he's not such a bad guy after all.

"Wait," Jeff calls. "It'll kill you even without its head." In the afternoon's furnace-like heat we hunker down and after making sure the snake is dead he starts to butcher and slice it into fleshy strips. "We could eat the head, too, if we extracted the venom sacs but I guess I shot all that poison to hell and gone."

Over a brushwood fire we barbecue the Mojave Green for dinner. I hated bivouacking in the army, but this is different, we're like injuns. *Ramis* or brothers in Comanche.

I hold up a piece of snake and slide it down my throat. Tastes like undercooked chicken. The country boy Texans in my outfit taught me how to sprinkle it with Tabasco sauce but we don't carry any. I'm still worried about the venom, but Jeff is chewing so I guess it's safe.

The sun goes down, and we haven't made motel arrangements. I guess we can sleep overnight in the Dodge. But, um, is he . . . ? No, never. Director Hoover would never allow it, he hates them even more than Communists if that's possible, and he won't even have women in the bureau.

I look through the dying campfire and realize Jeff is holding his .38 short barrel service gun on me. He's got it on half cock which means repeating fire if he pulls the trigger with a heavy squeeze. "Cleaning it," he explains, sighting along the barrel with both hands. But the cylinder is locked in place.

I move out of his sight line.

"You think I'm going to shoot you?" he laughs. He replaces the gun in a side holster that had been hidden by his Hawaiian shirt. "How about some target practice?" he suggests.

Jeff's idea of target practice is night shooting so he switches on the Dodge's headlights and offers me his gun to potshot at some yellow-flowered barrel cactus. I refuse, don't want my fingerprints on his weapon.

"Come on, soldier," he says.

We're out alone in the night desert.

He's pretty good with a .38 and blows the yellow flowers clean off the surrounding cactus in a circular Wyatt Earp bam-bam-bam hip swivel. The sounds are like cannon blasts in the cooling clean air. He reloads, and this time I take the offered weapon and aim but don't even get close. That's the trouble with the US army, they gave me a marksman medal like it was Halloween candy.

"Whyn't you go on over there and I bet I can put a hole in the dollar bill in your hand," he suggests.

I walk back to the fire to build it up with some dry cactus to get more light on our situation. We've both been drinking Jim Beam White Label, a cheap goyishe drink.

"Don't you trust me?" Jeff says. I say I don't even trust my mother in the dark.

"Yeah, nice lady. Very cooperative," and lifts the .38 and goes blam-blam-blam into the night.

That's it. Can't take my own fears anymore; I'm disgusted at how scared I am so much of the time. My reddening hands in the firelight look like a leper's. *Govno*, Ray would call it. Bullshit. Isn't there a limit?

I tell my creation, Buzz Law, I'm sleeping in the back of his Dodge and he can fire away all night if he likes. The long and short of it is, I do sleep in the car till midnight, he runs out of bullets, and we take turns driving back to LA in silence. As he lets me out at the Andalusia, he reaches across to open my door and says, "You be careful now, hear?"

57

You Bet Your Life

TERRY'S JOB AS a sound editor is to select the joke-appropriate chuckles, yocks, and guffaws on the Laff Track of Groucho Marx's immensely popular TV show, *You Bet Your Life*. No film editor is supposed to know the origin of the sweeteners they splice in, the canned laughter which is buried inside a secret electronic Laff Box patented by its mysterious inventor.

Groucho's show does have a real live audience capable of belching its own laughter but the producers don't trust humans to yock it up in the right places, hence a Laff Track machine programmed with a pre-existing armory of giggles, chuckles, titters, and guffaws recorded from other live audiences at other times in other shows. So the laugh you hear on Groucho's show may have first come from Red Skelton or Lucy. Laff tracks, with their cynical contempt for audiences, are comic McCarthyism.

I've come into Terry's editing cubicle to: say what? Express feelings unknown even to myself? A kiss goodbye?

Except she keeps interrupting me to stomp the pedal of the spool-equipped Movieola editing machine, running and rerunning artificial yocks timed to Groucho's jokes he reads off a bowling alley screen prompter offstage during the so-called live performance.

It goes like this:

"Ter—"

She hunches to peer into the Movieola's eyepiece. Groucho's smartass voice cracking through what I want to say:

"Ter, I—"

"WHO ARE YOU GOING TO BELIEVE, ME OR YOUR EYES . . . ?

"Look, I'm—"

". . . I MARRIED YOUR MOTHER BECAUSE I WANTED CHILDREN, IMAGINE MY DISAPPOINT-MENT WHEN YOU CAME ALONG . . ."

"I know that we've been—"

"YOU'VE GOT THE BRAIN OF A FOUR-YEAR-OLD BOY—AND I'LL BET HE WAS GLAD TO GET RID OF IT . . ."

She hardly glances at me as she synchronizes sound to image.

"What I mean is—"

"I'VE HAD A PERFECTLY WONDERFUL EVENING BUT THIS WASN'T IT . . ."

She's driving me nuts. Not for the first time.

"Look, can we talk . . . ?"

She concentrates fiercely on working the Movieola pedals, laying and overlaying sound tracks, judging which tired jokes deserve an audience rustle, roar, giggle, or just-so laugh. Overriding Groucho ("ONE MORNING I SHOT AN ELEPHANT IN MY PAJAMAS. HOW HE GOT INTO MY PAJAMAS I'LL NEVER KNOW . . .") she finally says, "I seem to remember those were my exact words when I came to your office!"

Oh, the Beauvoir fiasco.

I shout back over the canned audience, "Look, I just want to say—"

"Oh please," she twists a knob on the Movieola bringing up the sound to earsplitting level.

"WHY I'D HORSEWHIP YOU—IF I HAD A HORSE!"

That's when without warning she switches off the editing machine with its whirling spools as I shout into a sudden silence.

She perches on her editor's high stool gazing at me bemusedly. She has this way of cocking her head and looking at me sidewise. "It's awkward, isn't it, honey?" She's never called me honey before. Is this the woman for whom I applied the spermicide and fetched Tampax?

"I NEVER FORGET A FACE BUT IN YOUR CASE I'LL BE GLAD TO MAKE AN EXCEPTION!"

She's working the machine again. Un-be-lievable.

Ho ho ha ha haw haw! Canned laughter bursts from the machine as Terry goes back to work, timing the artificial sweeteners to my words.

I've lost her. How did this happen? She's in command. Before this, I was always in control, she liked it that way I believed. It never occurred to me that one day it would be otherwise.

A sledgehammer on my heart. I can hardly breathe.

"I WAS MARRIED BY A JUDGE. I SHOULD HAVE ASKED FOR A JURY!"

The joke is on me.

58

Dance, Girl, Dance

ON THE CLUB'S bandstand Pérez Prado is banging away on bongos, his trumpeters are shrieking his big hit "Cherry Pink and Apple Blossom White," and Ma and I are doing a fast-slow-fast mambo on the dance floor of La Bamba nightclub. The boisterous crowd is a mix of young and old, Mexican and yanqui, small-time dopers plus a few zoot suiters going wild around us, gyrating like crazy.

Ma is wearing her red-spangled dancing shoes, one of a dozen pairs in her closet, and I'm in a suit for the occasion, of this our last date for a while. Latin steps are not my thing, but Ma is a sensation in an ankle-length flowered dress split to the thigh for maneuverability. Hip teasing, waving her hands airily, shaking her hair like Hayworth's Gilda, she circles around me, waiting for my response. She's gorgeous tonight, slipping easily from mambo to cha-cha, her eyes sparkling with the beat.

She's wet with perspiration, even as we keep our mambo distance—no touch! We're alive to each other until she breaks the spell:

"So, big shot—will I ever see you again?"

She knows I'm all packed, everything I own in a GI duffel bag, and none of the Omegas wants my old car. It pains me that not even Goodwill or The Salvation Army will take it off my hands.

"It's not for forever," I promise.

"Don't kid a kidder. 'Not forever' is what your father told me before the earth swallowed him."

"Ma, I'm not him."

"So you say."

Cha cha.

She's tearing up, which rips me because Jennie never, ever cries in public.

"Ma."

"Come on, shake it, Sonny. It's my music."

Epilogue

F ROM OUTSIDE THE ship's saloon there are several blasts of the funnel's horn. The shy German boy with the burned hand comes over and says, "We are going now." Some of the passengers are at the portholes watching the dark shape of the dock slide by our passenger freighter, the *Haraklion* heading to Southampton, Le Havre, Rotterdam, and Hamburg, and I'll flip a coin to see where I get off.

I go out on deck. Slowly we swing into the Hudson River. I lean on the rail and watch New York City slip away. From my wallet I withdraw the scrap of paper, my insurance policy, on which are scrawled the **nine names** of the people I would have informed on.

I tear the list into shreds and toss them into the dark waters. Would I have? I'll never have the privilege of knowing.

THERE IS A terrific roaring and jamming and crackle coming from the ship's loudspeaker, and seeming to come from the reddish chrome and mirrors of the saloon. Out of the static come some very clear words, in English, in a halting foreign accent. *"This is Budapest. Budapest Radio. Budapest Radio. Help us. Help. Help. Help . . ."*

It's November 4, eleven days into an uprising by students and workers. Russian tanks penetrate Budapest, killing people as they go. Hungarian soldiers are deserting to the Resistance. Soviet forces overwhelm the defenders and take over Budapest Radio but not before a last, lone strangled cry: *"Budapest Radio. Budapest Radio. Help us. Help. Help . . ."*

It sounds as if they need a good agent.

Acknowledgments

ORKING ON THIS story I consulted with former Jaffe Agency personnel and others directly involved: Sam Jaffe and Mary Baker, Paul Jarrico, Bob Goldfarb, Evarts "Ziggy" Ziegler, Michael Ludmer, Ronnie Lubin, Swifty Lazar, Eleanor Kibbee, Lois Beckett Ursillo, Ed and Judith Bailey, and Jeff Lawson. Also agent Leslie Linder in London, and my close friend and competitor, agent-producer Alain Bernheim, formerly of the Charles Feldman agency.

Where Are They Now?

SAM JAFFE sold his agency to become a movie producer; on location in Africa he made *Born Free* about a lonely lion. After I moved to England we literally ran into each other in a London street demo outside the US embassy when baton-swinging mounted police chased me into Grosvenor Square where, at the foot of the bronze statue of President Franklin D. Roosevelt, I sent this elegant, elderly tourist gentleman sprawling. As I helped him to his feet he examined my dirty jeans, bovver boots, and anti-tear-gas bandana—normal anti-Vietnam war riot gear—and lamented, "Why does this not surprise me?" Later, when I re-emigrated to Los Angeles, I lived around the corner from him, and he liked touring us through his apartment showing off photographs of all the silent- and early sound-movie lovelies he had dated, like Clara Bow and Garbo.

MARY BAKER also retired to London and turned her vast energies to exhibiting collages in Bond Street art galleries. We regularly had dinner together. Bored in exile, Mary yearned to get back into the agent game. The last time Ava Gardner was there I couldn't stop gawping. Star-astigmatism strikes again: I was breaking bread not with a real person but with Honey Bear in John Ford's *Mogambo*.

PHIL GERSH created his own agency, which today is run by his sons.

"ZACK SILVER" and I remained longtime friends and poker partners; for a time he became my own agent, and helped me considerably with this book's research, as did "JONNY BUCK" who started his own agency and married several times. At our last lunch together, at the Polo Lounge, Jonny's current wife and two of his former wives were also there and seemed pleased to see him. Jonny was proud of the huge sums he had paid out in alimony. Mary's assistant CRICKET KENDALL and I became close once I left the agency; her daughter Eve Kendall gave her name to the role Eva Marie Saint plays in Hitchcock's *North by Northwest*, written by Jaffe client Ernest Lehman.

"RAY KOVACS" dropped from my life after outing himself as gay. He is one of several Communist homosexual friends who went into deep, permanent cover. I have never given up trying to find him.

TERRY I continued to see whenever I flew into Los Angeles from London.

Despite my best efforts PETER LORRE never escaped typecasting. DALE ROBERTSON retired to his ranch in

Yukon, Oklahoma. Our western "The Thousand Guns of Justin Molloy" remains unsold.

After the '65 Watts race riots, BUDD SCHULBERG launched the Watts Writers Workshop for African American writers. The Workshop was burned down by an FBI informer.

After *Rebel Without a Cause*, STEWART STERN had a successful screenwriting career. He lived in the Pacific Northwest where he led a support group of combat veterans with PTSD like himself.

My nemesis, the malignly powerful story editor RAY CROSSETT, who made it his life mission to destroy me as an agent, left Universal to become assistant to the mass-market novelist Harold Robbins. We reconciled.

Of the Ladies Auxiliary: One-eyed BOBETTE married her college sweetheart and I'd occasionally see her at class reunions. KELLY married an artist who adopted her two children. RHODA became pregnant by a man unknown to her, borrowed money from me for an abortion Barney arranged, and then disappeared. ANITA, who got me the Jaffe job, buried my mother JENNIE when I was unable to leave England for passport reasons; eventually her leopard skin bikini on the beach drew a man she then married and with whom she had three children. MAGGIE retired as a Los Angeles city librarian and never married. B-JAY married a rich lawyer, and as a divorcee and then widow became a financial angel for Broadway theater. I don't know what happened to ANNIE. MARCIA, the folk singer, married a man who beat her up, secluded her in the Valley without a car, and forced her to walk in the San Fernando heat while dragging a little red wagon behind her full of groceries and their infant boy. LAURA died soon after this story ends. None as far as I know ever turned me in to the FBI.

MUTT & JEFF, too, vanished but their reports keep resurfacing whenever the FBI reopens interest, especially when Jimmy Hoffa came into my life.

Of the Omegas that I know about: SPARKY retired from dock work and campaigned not for but against gun control; BARNEY is a therapist in the Bay Area; French horn player JOE became a symphony conductor in New England and never got over his anger at being blacklisted; DOROTHY went back east to care for her grandchild; JIMMY still works as a handyman day laborer; PETE became a high school counselor; "FRANK" the Communist or FBI spy— we never figured which—dropped out of sight.

BILL ALLAND died peacefully and without regrets.

Bride of the Gorilla can be rented on DVD.

I have searched unsuccessfully for years for the movie in which I play a dead Indian.

ABOUT THE AUTHOR

CLANCY SIGAL was a novelist, journalist, essayist, screenwriter and BBC commentator.

Born in Chicago to Jewish Russian union-organizer parents, he joined the Communist Party aged fifteen. Drafted in 1944, he served in occupied Germany, where he went AWOL on a quixotic solo mission to assassinate Hermann Goering at the Nuremberg Trials.

He studied in Los Angeles and, during the 'Second Red Scare', landed a job as a talent agent. Loathing the oppression of the time, he emigrated to Europe in 1957 to become a writer.

There he began a three-year romantic relationship with the writer Doris Lessing. His first novel, *Weekend in Dinlock* (1960) was based on his experience among a mining community in Yorkshire. *Going Away* (1961), a cross-country odyssey, was described in a *New York Times* review as being 'as if *On the Road* had been written by somebody with brains.' He was the inspiration for 'Saul Green' in Lessing's *The Golden Notebook* (1962).

Sigal was a patient and colleague of the 'anti-psychiatrist' R.D. Laing, with whom he set up Kingsley Hall, a radical experiment in treating schizophrenia. Fiercely political, Sigal returned to America to take part in the Civil Rights movement and later ran a London safe house for GI deserters from the Vietnam War.

From the 1980s he taught writing at the University of Southern California. With his wife, Janice Tidwell, he collaborated on screenplays, including the 2002 movie, *Frida*.

He died in July 2017, aged 90, shortly after finishing *Black Sunset*.

Photographs related to the events depicted in *Black Sunset* can be seen at www.clancysigal.com